WESTMINSTER CATHEDRAL

FROM DARKNESS TO LIGHT

WESTMINSTER CATHEDRAL
FROM DARKNESS TO LIGHT

PATRICK ROGERS

BURNS & OATES
A Continuum imprint
LONDON • NEW YORK

Burns and Oates
A Continuum imprint
The Tower Building
11 York Road
London SE1 7NX
www.continuumbooks.com

British Library cataloguing-in-Publication Data
A catalogue record for this book is available from the
British Library

ISBN 0 86012 358 8

Designed and typeset at Continuum
Printed and bound in Great Britain by Cromwell Press, Wiltshire

CONTENTS

CONTENTS

CONTENTS

FOREWORD

BY THE DUCHESS OF KENT

When the sun shines through the windows onto the blue mosaics high in the ceiling over the altar –

When a thousand candles flicker in the vast interior of the Cathedral during the Christmas celebration –

When the walls of this great Church tremble and the air vibrates to the sound of the organ –

When from the distant choir stalls the voices of the choristers soar up to the dark vaults of the ceiling above –

When humility, awe and a deep sense of the presence of God fills your soul each time you enter this magnificent building –

When the noisy outside world fades into insignificance –

This is Westminster Cathedral in all its magnificence, solemnity and pageantry. A home to many – a place of refuge to others.

One symbol – in the centre of London – of the length and breadth of the Catholic community thoughout the world.

Where prayer crosses every boundary and arms stretch out across the globe in a gesture of peace and understanding.

Katharine Kent

The Duchess of Kent

PREFACE

BY HIS EMINENCE CARDINAL MURPHY-O'CONNOR

Westminster Cathedral speaks to me very personally of two things which may often seem to be in tension in our lives, the first of which is contemplation. In Word, in sacrament, in music, and in silence the Cathedral invites us to spend time in contemplation of the mystery of the Incarnation – God's gift of Himself to us in the person of Jesus Christ. In this place our minds, our hearts and our deepest yearnings can be raised up to God. And I hope that anyone and everyone who comes here will feel moved by the Spirit of God whose home this is.

The second is the importance we, as followers of Jesus, are asked to attach not only to prayer and contemplation, but also to action. We are asked to build the Kingdom of God not just in the privacy of our hearts, but in the public place which is the world in which we live. Ours is not a private faith. It is a universal faith lived in the midst of, and for the sake of, all men and women.

It is not by chance that the Cathedral is best seen by entering the great doors which open into the Cathedral from the piazza. This Cathedral is intended to be a sign of the presence of God in our midst, accessible to everyone who feels moved to come inside. I hope and pray that in an age when people are searching everywhere for God many, many will find Him here.

Archbishop of Westminster

PROLOGUE

BY SIR ROY STRONG

My first awareness of Westminster Cathedral is a somewhat eccentric one. In Alfred Hitchcock's thriller *Foreign Correspondent* there is a sequence on the balcony of the Cathedral's tower. A murder attempt is made as someone rushes to push the luckless victim off its summit. Somehow the latter, I recall, either steps or is pulled to one side at the last minute and it is the assailant who plunges to his fate. So my first awareness of Bentley's masterpiece was on celluloid.

The Cathedral was not to enter my consciousness again until 1968 when, shortly after I was appointed Director of the National Portrait Gallery, I moved into the first of two flats in Morpeth Terrace immediately to the right of the Cathedral's facade. From these I have contemplated the entire length of its south side for almost four decades in all weathers and at every season of the year. The first flat was occupied in the Victorian period by the artist, Hercules Brabazon Brabazon and, after I became Director of the Victoria & Albert Museum in 1974 I was delighted to discover that the Prints & Drawings Department held watercolours by him looking from the flat's windows over to the Cathedral's predecessor, the Middlesex County Prison. Those four decades have seen many changes, not only physical ones to the area in which the Cathedral is sited, but also in attitude both to its architecture and decoration. That reassessment began particularly after the entrance facade was opened up to Victoria Street. Suddenly a great architectural masterpiece, hitherto hidden, was not only revealed but displayed to advantage for the very first time. In recent years too that sense of revelation has been heightened by the cleaning of the exterior, drawing attention to the sophisticated articulation of its surfaces as they pass from brick to stone. Both these materials surprise as does the Cathedral's style, Byzantine.

Cholera, in Istanbul, prevented the architect ever going there but I find it difficult to believe that he had not studied pictures of the interior of Hagia Sophia. Both churches are about the creation of a vast sacred space inbued with a sense of mystery and holiness. I always pause on entering the Cathedral to reflect on that as Bentley's supreme achievement.

Within, the eye is next taken by the pleasing contrast between the modest workmanlike brick and where it has been lined with rich marbles and mosaics. Add to that a striking stylistic unity in its decoration. This Cathedral was open for public worship only eight years after its foundation stone was laid. What a contrast to its sister along Victoria Street, Westminster Abbey, whose present building was begun in the middle of the thirteenth century and only finished in the eighteenth.

So what Westminster Cathedral can rejoice in is its youth. It is as yet less burdened with the luggage of the past. It has only begun to gather history to itself, a process which simultaneously enhances, but equally can paralyse any great building. The challenge for the twenty first century will be to ensure that the Cathedral is not paralysed by its past but rather enhanced to by it for the great role of service it has to play to the whole Christian community of this country.

Roy Strong

INTRODUCTION

Although opening with a description of the prison which stood where Westminster Cathedral now stands, this book is not about the building of the Cathedral. That was comprehensively described in 1919 by Winefride de l'Hôpital in *Westminster Cathedral and its Architect* and in 1995 by John Browne and Tim Dean in *Westminster Cathedral: Building of Faith*. Instead it focuses on the decoration of the Cathedral which has taken place over the last 100 years and is still continuing today.

Similarly it does not provide a guided tour of the Cathedral, chapel by chapel, for once again this can be found in the books of 1919 and 1995 and, more briefly, in the many guidebooks available. Instead it examines particular features – the successes, the mistakes and the controversies. It is also about people, some of them almost unknown, who played a key role in the decoration of the Cathedral. People such as the unsung architect John Marshall, the marble merchant and explorer William Brindley, and artists such as Robert Anning Bell, Eric Gill, Gilbert Pownall, Boris Anrep and Aelred Bartlett.

Particular attention is given to the Cathedral marbles, for our 125 varieties almost certainly represent the largest collection in England outside a museum. Many of these marbles come from quarries used by the Greeks and Romans, some of them rediscovered and reopened to supply the Cathedral. Indeed some of the panels we see on the walls and floor of the Cathedral today originally adorned the buildings of Rome and its empire. The marble merchants who decorated the Cathedral were the best in England and no better display of 'book-matched' cipollino, for example, can be found in this country.

Visitors to the Cathedral often ask questions – many of them unanswered in the guidebooks. Some of the most common are: What was here before? Was there any war damage? How many marbles are there? Why do the mosaics look different? Who uses those balconies? Is that a real body? What did the monkey look like? By going through the Cathedral records and architectural drawings, together with the press reports of the time, and by speaking to those who still remember what really happened, an attempt has been made to answer at least some of those questions.

The last chapter provides pen-portraits of the first nine Cardinal Archbishops of Westminster, together with the main events in the building and decoration of the Cathedral over which they presided. This is followed by a brief word, a postscript really, about those who recorded the life and times of the Cathedral over the last 100 years, in *Oremus* and its predecessors.

My thanks to Tanis Kent, who came with me on many research expeditions, to Joan Bond of the Catholic Central Library, and Evaline Brown of the Cathedral archives, to Aelred Bartlett, Jane Buxton (Gilbert Pownall's daughter) and John Skelton (Eric Gill's nephew); to marble merchants Gerald Culliford, Ian MacDonald of

McMarmilloyd, Tsalmas Melas of Tsalma Marble, Larissa, Greece, and Ambrose Joyce (father and son) of Connemara Marble Industries, Moycullen, Galway; to Roman marble expert Monica Price at Oxford University Natural History Museum, Mike Dorling at the Sedgwick Museum of Geology at Cambridge and Henry Buckley and Dave Smith at the Natural History Museum in London; to Matthew Parkes of the Geological Survey of Ireland, Dublin, Tom Heldal of the Geological Survey of Norway, Trondheim, and Ian Thomas, Director of the National Stone Centre, Wirksworth, Derbyshire; to Tessa Hunkin of Mosaic Workshop, London, Sheree Leeds of Surrey House, Norwich, and Anne Milton of the RC National Shrine Pilgrim Bureau, Walsingham; to Catriona Allan of Cnoc a' Chalmain, Isle of Iona; to Fr Michael Seed sa and to my colleagues on *Oremus* (the magazine of Westminster Cathedral), particularly Fr Richard Andrew, Joseph Bonner and Elizabeth Benjamin, who put the whole thing together.

Patrick Rogers
Spring 2003

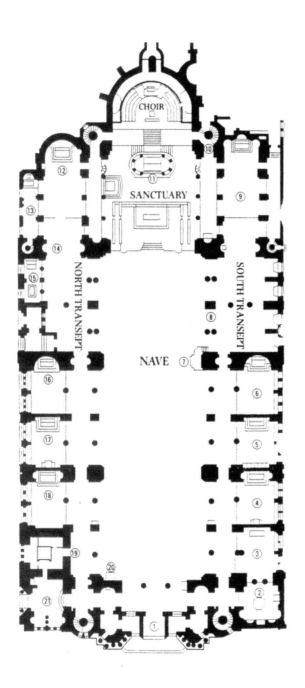

Plan of Westminster Cathedral

1 Main entrance
2 Baptistry
3 Chapel of St Gregory and St Augustine
4 Chapel of St Patrick
5 Chapel of St Andrew
6 Chapel of St Paul
7 Pulpit
8 Shrine of Our Lady of Westminster
9 Lady Chapel
10 Entrance to crypt
11 High Altar
12 Chapel of the Blessed Sacrament
13 Sacred Heart shrine
14 Peacock and phoenix mosaics
15 Chapel of St Thomas of Canterbury (Cardinal
   Vaughan chantry)
16 Chapel of St Joseph
17 Chapel of St George and the English Martyrs
18 Chapel of the Holy Souls
19 Entrance to the campanile
20 Statue of St Peter
21 Giftshop

CREATION AND SURVIVAL
BEFORE THE CATHEDRAL

'That land is for sale, I wish you to buy it.' Cardinal Manning was addressing his solicitor, Alfred Blount, in November 1882. What both men were looking at, from the cardinal's residence at the bottom of Carlisle Place, was Tothill Fields Prison. Blount formed a company and bought the site in 1884. The western half was immediately sold to the cardinal at cost, the remainder to a property developer. On the land sold to the cardinal now stands Westminster Cathedral.

Tothill Fields Prison was formally entitled the Middlesex (Westminster) House of Correction. Established by Act of Parliament in 1826, it opened in 1834. It was designed on enlightened, Benthamite principles and built on an eight-acre site of open ground, now enclosed by Morpeth Terrace to the west, Francis Street to the south and east, and Ashley Place and Howick Place to the north. From 1618 a much smaller prison, Tothill Fields Bridewell, had stood immediately north of Greencoat School (now a pub) and west of Artillery Row. It was knocked down in 1836, two years after the new prison opened, and the site is now occupied by shops and the Army and Navy Stores.

The Tothill Fields Prison of 1834 was built in the form of a shamrock or ace of clubs, each 'leaf' effectively forming a separate prison, with a planted courtyard in the centre and exercise yards beside each brick-built cell block. The main entrance, of massive granite blocks with iron gates, opened onto Francis Street. North of the planted courtyard was the prison governor's house surmounted by a chapel. 'Vast, airy, light and inexorably safe', only one inmate escaped from the prison, when the door-keeper absentmindedly laid down his key.

Initially for both men and women with sentences less severe than transportation, from 1850 it was restricted to convicted female prisoners and males below 17 years. Each of the three prison 'leaves' contained about 300 prisoners, the one on the left for the boys and the other two for women. Westminster Cathedral, Clergy House and the Choir School now stand on the site of the boys' wing and a part of one of those occupied by the women. The rest of the prison complex now lies beneath Ambrosden Avenue, Ashley Gardens and Thirleby Road.

We know much about the prison from Henry Mayhew's *Criminal Prisons of London*, written after a visit there in 1861. It operated on the 'silent associated' system in which inmates mixed but were not allowed to talk among themselves. Of course they did and it is significant that by far the main punishment was restriction of diet (usually for talking). The most serious punishment, whipping, had only been inflicted twice in the five years 1851-5, considerably less than elsewhere. Mayhew wrote that the staff of the boys' prison were entitled to the highest praise, enforcing strict discipline with a minimum of physical coercion.

The oldest boy in 1861 was 18, having lied about his age to get in. A number were aged six and one as young as five, having stolen 5/9d from a till (his second offence). But the great majority were 14-16-year-olds. Almost all had no trade or occupation and most could not read or write. On arrival the boys were given a bath and a meal and issued with the prison uniform of a tricolour striped woollen cap with earflaps (used also as a night-cap in the unheated cells), an iron grey (prison blue for minor offenders), three-piece suit without pockets, check shirt, stock, boots and a small red cotton handkerchief to be tied to a buttonhole.

The boys were identified by numbers on the left arm. A yellow number 1 identified the 1st-class – sentenced to more than three months, a 2 denoted a sentence of between 14 days and three months (2nd-class), while 3rd-class inmates (14 days or less) bore no number. A badge was worn for a sentence of two years or more, a yellow ring around the arm denoted penal servitude and a yellow waistcoat collar committal for larceny or felony. Also worn, often proudly, was a red number revealing how many times they had been imprisoned before, one 14-year-old as many as 17.

The boys were awakened by a gun at 6.25am. Then followed a communal wash in cold water, Chapel and breakfast of oatmeal gruel (porridge), bread and water, the basic diet at all three meals. Most then worked at oakum picking (unravelling rope for use in caulking the seams of vessels). Other work consisted of mending clothes and shoes, carpentry and gardening. An hour was spent in exercise and another in the schoolroom. At midday dinner the 2nd-class prisoners received tinned cold meat (beef or mutton) with potatoes twice a week and oxhead, barley and vegetable soup twice a week, while the 1st-class received this superior diet (and cocoa at breakfast) six days out of the seven. Lock-up was at 6pm.

Most were in for theft, over a third for picking pockets. As one boy put it 'I seem to like thieving'. But others were there for knocking at doors and running away, an eight year-old had been sentenced to 14 days and a flogging for taking some half-dozen plums from an orchard, and boys aged ten and eleven were there for spinning a top! Nearly half were recommittals (against 25 per cent nationally). One youth was suspected of throwing stones at a street lamp just to get a month's shelter. Many were fending for themselves on the streets of London. They looked on the prison as a place where they would at least be given shelter, food and warm clothing. Indeed Mayhew was prevented from using a drawing of the boys at breakfast as it would have made the place seem far too comfortable!

Mayhew described the part of the prison occupied by the women in less detail. They wore close white caps with deep frills and loose blue and white spotted dresses. They wore the same identifying numbers as the boys and, like them, longer-term prisoners received the better diet. Over half were recommittals, many for non-payment of fines. One girl of eight had been sentenced to three months for stealing a pair of boots. When asked why she replied 'I hadn't got none of my own'. Besides oakum picking, there was straw plaiting, knitting and laundry work. There were two schoolrooms, one of them for girls of up to 16, and a nursery where those with young children could look after them when not working.

So why did Tothill Fields Prison, well-built and well-run, close after less than 50 years? Two reasons, I think. Firstly it was not an effective deterrent. Recommittals were twice the number elsewhere and some seemed happy to return. The regime was strict rather than harsh and those released often went out into a harsher and less secure world. The prison was enlightened and enlightenment can be expensive. The cost per prisoner at Tothill was a third more than at Coldbath Fields House of Correction, Clerkenwell. But if the prison had not been built where and when it was, or if, perhaps, its regime had been harsher and more cost effective, Westminster Cathedral would not stand where it does today.

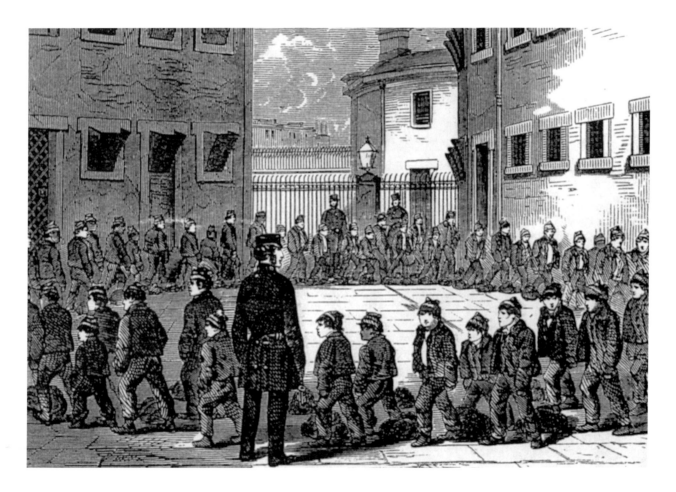

Boys exercising while in Tothill Fields Prison.

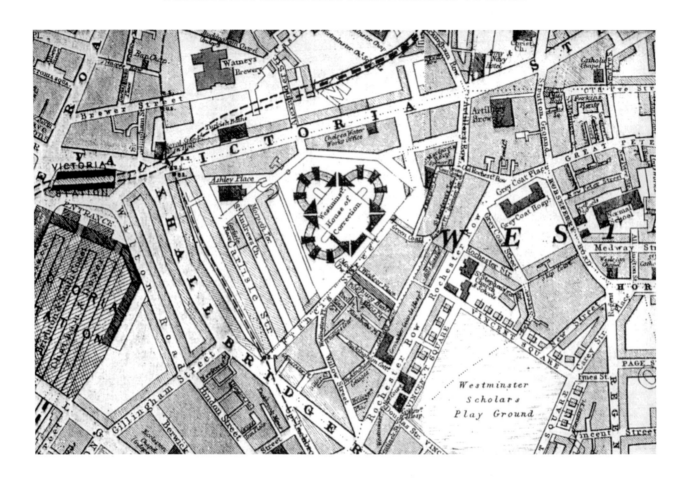

Bird's-eye view of Tothill Fields Prison in 1883

THE CHOIR THAT NEVER WAS

When visitors are taken up behind the high altar into the apse of the Cathedral, where the choir sings, they see a little balcony on either side, each decorated with twin marble columns and glittering mosaic. Not surprisingly they ask who uses them. The short answer is that they contain electrical equipment and are otherwise unused. But for their original purpose we have to go back over 100 years.

Cardinal Herbert Vaughan, founder of Westminster Cathedral, came from a recusant family and had a strong sense of history. Right from the first he saw the new building as a means of providing the congregation with the daily Divine Office in its entirety, a practice long since abandoned as part of public worship in this country. The body he chose to carry this out were English Benedictines, expelled from Westminster Abbey at the Reformation, for besides their return appealing to his sense of history, he believed that no other body of men could present the Divine Liturgy so reverently and effectively.

Thus it was that when John Francis Bentley, the Cathedral architect, started work in 1895, his plans included a Benedictine monastery, a large chapel for the monks and an extensive area behind the altar for a Benedictine choir. Meanwhile, as the first step in bringing the monks back to London, in May 1896 Vaughan contacted Downside Abbey and offered them a mission at Ealing (to the indignation of the incumbent priest, who refused to leave). The new Benedictine monastery would serve both the pastoral needs of local Catholics and provide a community of monks on which the Cathedral could draw when the time came. Downside accepted his proposals, the Monastery of St Benedict's, Ealing, was founded in 1897 and building started two years later.

But then the cardinal began to get second thoughts. English Benedictines were unusual in that they did not live a truly monastic life but were at that time bound by a missionary oath to work in a pastoral capacity in their missions or parishes. Almost inevitably such work would lead to clashes with the secular clergy if it took place at the Cathedral. Were there any other Benedictines who could sing the Divine Office without being bound to a missionary commitment? Thus it was that Cardinal Vaughan took the surprising step of offering the position already offered to English Benedictines to the French Benedictines of Solesmes Abbey, who were truly monastic and were renowned for their plainsong.

The response of Solesmes was favourable. They envisaged a French-controlled monastery at Westminster with rooms for 30 French monks. But for the first year of a three-year trial period they could supply only about 15, not all of them with good voices. Could the English Benedictines help by bringing the number up to 20? Thus in late 1900 Vaughan was forced to return to the English Benedictines to ask them to assist in the establishment of a French Benedictine community at Westminster Cathedral. The proposal was regarded as an insult. In February 1901 the President of the General Chapter of English Benedictines wrote to Vaughan refusing to countenance foreign Benedictines at Westminster. Without such agreement Vaughan knew he could not proceed and regretfully wrote to the French accordingly.

In an attempt to defuse the ill feeling which the issue by now had engendered, both between English and French Benedictines and between them and the secular clergy, the Benedictine president suggested that secular priests should undertake the liturgy at the Cathedral and that a choir school be formed. And so, with a mixture of regret and relief, Vaughan abandoned his plan for a return of Benedictine monks to Westminster and turned to the secular clergy. At the Diocesan Synod of 1901 he announced the change of plan and called on them to provide the high standard of church music required. At the same time the formation of a choir school was announced. The response was enthusiastic.

On Ascension Day 1902 the entire Divine Office and High Mass were sung for the first time by the new choir of the Cathedral. The friction which had arisen between Benedictines and secular clergy over the issue gradually dissipated and in 1976 George Basil Hume, Benedictine Abbot of Ampleforth, was appointed Archbishop of Westminster. Four years later, to commemorate the 1,500th anniversary of St Benedict's birth, more than 400 Benedictine monks and nuns attended a special Mass in the Cathedral, afterwards walking to Westminster Abbey to sing vespers.

So what remains today of Vaughan's romantic dream? Ealing Abbey became a priory in 1916 and an abbey in 1955 and serves a large parish. A school, started in 1902, caters for some 600 senior pupils and 250 juniors. In the Cathedral it is to Vaughan's plan for a Benedictine choir that we owe the excellent acoustics from the raised, six-windowed retro-choir behind the high altar, designed to provide the space and light needed for the monks to sing the Divine Office. At the back, and still used, are twin oak doors for the monks to process across a bridge, along the cloisters (now Long Corridor) to the monastery (now the Choir School).

And the two little balconies, glittering with mosaic? Attractive in themselves, they provide a perfect view of the retro-choir below while allowing any occupant to remain unseen from public gaze. That on the right is a one-minute walk from Archbishop's House, via the Library and Long Corridor. I suggest that it was for the use of Cardinal Vaughan, who was devoted to the Divine Office but would have been loath to cause distraction by appearing in public. The balcony on the left is necessary for symmetry and could also have been used by senior visitors and perhaps Benedictines not directly involved in the liturgy below. Support for this theory is provided by Vaughan's occupation of a similar private oratory when attending Divine Office in the Cathedral hall. This was located on the upper gallery at the back of the hall, access being through the private library in Archbishop's House.

THE LOST SEA OF WESTMINSTER

The main players in this historical drama are a cardinal in a hurry, an architect who knew that time was running out for him and another architect with an eye for a bargain. The action takes place 100 years ago in south west London and Norwich.

In the summer of 1901 Cardinal Vaughan was a disappointed man. The thirteenth centenary of St Augustine's landing had come and gone. So had the Golden Jubilee of the Restoration of the Catholic Hierarchy, on 29 September 1900 – a date provisionally fixed for the Cathedral's consecration and opening. Yet the building was unfinished. Writing in *The Tablet* in June 1902 the cardinal sadly explained that a further £16,000 was still required for work to be completed and to pay off liabilities. Under Canon Law a church must be free of debt before consecration can take place.

Meanwhile, J F Bentley was working impossible hours. Since starting on the Cathedral in 1895 he had suffered two paralytic strokes -- the first in late 1898 and a more serious one in the summer of 1900. He had experienced considerable disappointment when the cardinal had overruled him – ordering what Bentley regarded as an unsuitable altar of unadorned Cornish granite, Algerian onyx columns (subsequently rejected) for the baldacchino, and a pulpit and throne made in Rome. Knowing that time was running out for him, Bentley rapidly laid down a scheme for the marble revetment of the nave, sanctuary and side chapels. But his main concern was the floor.

Bentley's plan for the nave floor consisted of wave-like cipollino marble inset with many types of fish – an allusion to the Church as a ship carrying the faithful over the troubled sea of life. His designs show the floor divided into 10ft x 9ft sections, each containing five waved bands with inlaid fish. Alternate compartments of light grey marble framed by small black and white squares are interspersed at regular intervals by pink or blue tesserae set in a ground of golden yellow, all enclosed within a 9in dark marble border. Each 10ft panel is divided from its neighbour by a 2ft 9in strip of light marble running the length of each bay. Between bays in the breadth of the piers are 4ft circles of rose-red marble, alternating with lozenges of green enclosed in tesserae-filled squares of equal diameter.

'What a grand floor!' wrote Cardinal Vaughan when the design finally reached him in October 1901 and promptly had it costed. The estimate was £1 per square foot or £15,000 for the whole area. This would have doubled the debt on the Cathedral to £31,000 (£1.3 million today) and would have postponed consecration indefinitely. To Bentley's dismay the cardinal cancelled the scheme. Writing after the architect's death a few months later, he justified his decision on the grounds of cold, damp and the noise of chairs scraping on the marble. But it is clear that the overriding factor was economic. Some concession was made in 1903 in the shape of marble paving (to Bentley's designs) of the main entrance narthex and between the piers and columns. But the nave was fitted out with wood-block flooring.

Now the scene switches to Norwich, to the boardroom of the Norwich Union Life Insurance Society on 6 December 1901. George Skipper, architect for Surrey House, the company's new head offices, announces to the directors that a large consignment of very fine marble ordered for Westminster Cathedral has unexpectedly become available. A strike in the Italian quarries has resulted in it arriving too late to be used there. Skipper had inspected the marble and provided samples. The interior of Surrey House could be fitted out with it at the bargain price of £8,139. The board approved. The marble was bought, decoration proceeded and Surrey House was completed and occupied in 1904.

Surrey House is now a cornucopia of polished marble – and what marble! Column after column – six in the vestibule, 40 more in the 60ft x 60ft marble hall – more main columns than in the whole of the Cathedral but in a fraction of the space. Slab after slab on the walls and galleries, many of them 2in thick; the columns in light green Greek cipollino, very strikingly patterned, together with dark green verde antico, Greek rosso antico, and lighter red Skyros on the 30ft-high walls. Also on the walls, staircases and floor are Italian varieties – pink and white alabaster, violet breccia, grey bardiglio, white veined pavonazzo and white statuary from Carrara. Particularly attractive are the eight little pillars of rare yellow Siena which support the air fountain in the centre of the hall.

The marbles which suddenly came onto the market at the end of 1901 closely resemble those intended by Bentley for his marble sea. The huge amount of wavy green cipollino, smaller quantities of verde antico, rosso antico, Skyros, Siena, bardiglio and the rest would have served him very well. The existing paving of the Cathedral's entrance narthex and that between the columns and piers employ virtually the same marbles. The explanation of a delayed marble shipment in 1901 is unconvincing. The Cathedral's structural nave columns were in place by December 1900 and decorative marble work did not start until 1902.

We will never know for sure what happened 100 years ago and how the marble unexpectedly became available. As a pamphlet on Skipper's firm of architects put it in 1980, 'The reasons have never been adequately elucidated'. The firm of Farmer and Brindley, which undertook the marble work in Surrey House, was one which did much of the work (including the paving) in the Cathedral. Clearly they had excess stock, quite probably resulting in cash-flow and storage problems. They could well have imported the marble on Bentley's instructions. It seems very likely that Bentley, knowing that after two strokes the sands were running out for him, and determined to supervise as much of the work in the Cathedral as he could, went ahead and ordered the marble for his sea in the expectation that it would be approved. As the cardinal was later to write 'Mr Bentley was a poet; he cared little for economy.' The cardinal's decision must have come as a bitter blow.

Another, not incompatible, explanation may relate to the fact that Farmer and Brindley missed out on another major contract at this time. Edward Mountford had been chosen as architect for the new Old Bailey courthouse following a competition in 1898. The first stone was laid in 1902 and the building opened in 1907. Inside, the two great halls and connecting stairway are lined with marble, including a large number of Greek verde antico and cipollino columns similar in size and appearance to those now in Surrey House. Farmer and Brindley, the leading marble merchants in London at the time, may well have assumed that the Old Bailey marblework contract was theirs, and ordered the stock which would be needed – particularly column blocks. In the event it was another firm, Arthur Lee of Hayes, Middlesex, which secured the contract.

So what would the Cathedral's marble sea have looked like? Bentley's drawings, his marble floor in the narthex, and the fish and other sea creatures on the floor of St Andrew's Chapel, can give us some idea, though only a very limited one. For the rest we can only imagine.

Bentley's plan for the marble floor of the Cathedral

THE GREAT ROOD

Passers-by on Victoria Street see the Cathedral and often wonder what it is and what it looks like inside. Many of them come in to find out. The first thing they see is likely to be the body of a man on a great red and gold cross, and at once they know they are in a Christian church.

The crucifix or Great Rood (from the Old English rod meaning cross) was designed by architect J F Bentley soon after starting work on the Cathedral in 1895. A drawing signed by him (A8) and dated 1896 shows it hanging in its present position. The scale below the drawing shows the rood dimensions (30ft x 23ft) to be the same as they are today, while the figure of Christ also seems identical. Differences now are the absence of the five great hanging lamps and in the end panel paintings. In the drawing these show the dove of the Holy Spirit (above), the Lamb of God (below) and Our Lady and St John to left and right. Today they show the symbols of the four evangelists who described the crucifixion – Matthew (an angel), Mark (a lion), Luke (an ox) and John (an eagle).

Cardinal Vaughan was directly involved with the rood, writing in 1903 to William Christian Symons, who was to paint it, that the representation must be of the living Christ – there must be no pierced side. In this he seems to have been thinking of crucifixes made from the sixth to the thirteenth centuries which portray a living, triumphant Christ. Vaughan's views also appeared in the last issue of the *Westminster Cathedral Record*, published as a supplement to *The Tablet* in June 1902. This confirms the height (30ft) of the rood and its position (to hang between the sanctuary and nave), and refers to the paintings of the four evangelists in the end panels and of Our Lady of Sorrows (Mater Dolorosa) on the reverse side.

By this time the rood was being carved in Bruges from Bentley's designs. Canvas was then stretched over the teak and deal frame and Symons painted it in the Cathedral in 1903, from sketches seen by Bentley before his death in March 1902. In portraying the dead Christ, Symons remained faithful to Bentley's design, but the evangelists and Our Lady of Sorrows were portrayed as the cardinal wished. Vaughan also chose the quotations from the Stabat Mater for the end panels around Our Lady. These are taken from a late thirteenth-century Latin hymn by a Franciscan, Jacopone di Todi. The English version of the hymn starts: 'At the cross her station keeping, stood the mournful mother weeping.' The words in the panels may be translated as: 'Stood the sorrowful mother; O Mother, fount of love; Make my heart to burn in me; Beside the cross to stand with Thee.'

Once the painting was complete the two-ton cross was hauled into position over a period of several hours. And there it remained for 30 years while the liturgies and decoration of the Cathedral took place below. But a new cardinal, Francis Bourne, had succeeded Vaughan and in 1932-3 the arch between the sanctuary and apse, behind the rood, was decorated with a great blue mosaic of Christ in Majesty. Bourne found that the Great Rood obscured this and late in 1933 he had it removed to a position in the north-west corner of the nave – above the bronze plaque listing the names of the Chief

The rood after being painted in 1903

Pastors of the church. High on the wall there you can still see the four steel girders which supported it.

In his New Year message to the *Cathedral Chronicle* of January 1934, Cardinal Bourne explained his decision on the grounds that Bentley had originally planned a much smaller cross to hang over the baldacchino, that the Great Rood was an afterthought, miscalculated in preparation and out of proportion. In this he seems to have been repeating Winifride de l'Hôpital, in *Westminster Cathedral and its Architect* (published 1919), that due to an error in measurement the rood's proportions were not exactly as Bentley intended. But both Bourne and de l'Hôpital seem to have been mistaken, or the error was a relatively minor one. The 1902 *Cathedral Record* and Bentley's drawings A8 and F84 (the rood frame) show the position and dimensions of the rood as they are today. Bentley and Cardinal Vaughan clearly gave it much thought and Bentley was meticulous in his drawings and directions.

An article by Bentley in the *Cathedral Record* of January 1896 shows that he initially planned to hang both a gilt cross and a painted crucifix about 30ft high (the Great Rood). Bentley's drawings give no sign of plans for a cross to hang over the baldacchino, but three drawings (B24, 26, 34) show a bronze gilt cross, only 20in high, mounted on top of it. The *Cathedral Record* of June 1902 also refers to the baldacchino 'surmounted by a cross'. In any event Bentley's death, the arrival of broken baldacchino columns, and the subsequent death of the cardinal in June 1903, appear to have disrupted plans. Neither in a drawing of the baldacchino received in 1904 by the marble merchants (Farmer and Brindley), nor on the baldacchino itself, erected by them in 1906, is there any sign of the little bronze cross.

In Bourne's 1934 New Year message he explained that the new mosaic of Christ in Majesty was intended to recall the dedication of the Cathedral (to the Precious Blood) and was inspired by the Church of which he was titular bishop, Santa Pudenziana in Rome. In this church a graceful fourth-century apse mosaic, the oldest in Rome, dominates the nave. Above the central figure of Christ enthroned appears a great jewelled mosaic cross, similar to that in the Blessed Sacrament Chapel here. After this it was clearly galling to Bourne to have his own sanctuary mosaic in the Cathedral obscured by a 30ft high painted rood. In the event, one of the first recommendations of the Cathedral Advisory Art Committee, set up after Bourne's death in 1935, was that the Great Rood be restored to its old position. In February 1937 it was.

The Great Rood has now hung undisturbed for 66 years while, once again, the liturgies and decoration of the Cathedral have proceeded below. The rood is the focal point of the Cathedral. Without it there would be a vacuum at the centre. In the last issue of the *Cathedral Record* in June 1902 (in effect the voice of Cardinal Vaughan) it was forecast that the Great Rood would 'dominate the whole Cathedral by its majestic presence, and it will be the first object to catch the eye on entering. This is as it should be – Christus vincit, Christus regnat, Christus imperat.' It does, it is and it should.

LET THERE BE LIGHT

Providing appropriate lighting in a neo-Byzantine building the size of Westminster Cathedral posed very real problems both for the architect, John Bentley, and for his successor, John Marshall. Whether or not they succeeded is a matter which only those using the Cathedral can judge.

Internally the Cathedral is 342ft long by 148ft wide and is surmounted by four shallow domes rising to 112ft, the last of these, above the sanctuary, being somewhat lower. Bentley's objective was to provide sufficient daylight without putting in long rows of identical windows which could have made the building look like a factory. So he decided to use two very different styles of windows, not always arranged in the same way and with a series of different patterns for the tracery and glazing. He chose a greenish glass, conscious that future decoration with mosaic and coloured marble would make anything approaching stained glass both unnecessary and inappropriate. But he had to override the objections of Cardinal Vaughan who wanted something warmer in effect.

Looking first above the main entrance doors, the head (tympanum) of the arch here is filled with a great horizontal semicircle of terracotta tracery, tailor-made by Doulton of Lambeth. Enclosed within this framework are leaded glass panels of tinted glass, arranged to resemble flowers. Below this great window Bentley inserted three contrasting vertical windows, round-headed and filled with serried ranks of lead-framed Venetian roundels or 'bull's-eyes'. Though there are variations, including a few small, round windows, these are essentially the two styles chosen by Bentley for the main windows of the Cathedral.

Bentley wanted to break up the featureless expanse of the great arches on each side of the nave, which are essential to support the domes. So he built a pair of smaller, coupled arches into each one. Into the head of all but one of these new arches went a semicircular window of terracotta, of alternating pattern, with the enclosed glass panels forming fleur-de-lys and other flowers. Below it went a pair of the vertical round-headed windows with 'bull's-eye' glass, each containing a decorated panel different from its neighbour. Only below the third dome, where the nave meets the transepts, is this scheme varied. Here the semicircular terracotta window is absent and there is a triangle of three vertical round-headed windows.

The sanctuary also has a semicircular window of terracotta at the head of the arch on either side, with a pair of vertical round-headed windows below. But the drum of the shallow dome above is itself pierced by a circle of 12 round-headed windows to provide additional light for this, the focal point of the Cathedral. Behind the sanctuary, the apse, which Bentley understood was to be used for the singing of the Divine Office, is amply provided with six round-headed windows facing east. Finally twin recesses in the side chapels each enclose two or three windows containing leaded and patterned glass. Perhaps most attractive are the flower-like patterns in the Holy Souls Chapel, and St Andrew's, where the white cross of the saint appears on an azure blue ground.

Bentley died in 1902, before the Cathedral was complete, and it fell to his successor, John Marshall, to design the artificial lighting. The 12 great electric light pendants in the nave were made by Singers of Frome of wrought iron. Although put in place in early 1909, they were not used until 1912 when their cost of £2,005 (about £80,000 today) was finally met. They resemble descriptions of the circular pendants which carried oil lamps in Justinian's sixth-century Byzantine church of Santa Sophia in Constantinople. The top ring is 6ft in diameter and carries 15 lamps, the next bears ten and the lowest and smallest three, each ring being independently controlled. The six pendants in the sanctuary follow a similar design but are considerably smaller and gilt.

The Byzantine-style lighting of the Lady Chapel consists of eight chandeliers of silvered copper suspended from bronze cantilevers. Each is in the form of a corona or crown, pierced and decorated, and suspended from a star. Below hang medallions pierced with fleur-de-lis and bearing four electric lamps, with a fifth in the centre attached to an oval medallion displaying Our Lady's monogram. On the other side of the Cathedral the eight light pendants in the Blessed Sacrament Chapel are very different, being in the form of bronze gilt diamonds, pierced and enamelled with alpha and omega symbols and coloured diamonds. They carry five electric lights, the lowest attached to a cross. The three silver oil lamps suspended before the tabernacle are decorated with blue and green enamel and set with onyx and rock crystal.

Next door in the Shrine of the Sacred Heart, beams carry four silvered bronze pendants in the form of a cross, each bearing a single light. The oil lamp before the statue was designed by Osmund Bentley, the architect's son. At the other end of the Cathedral, the four light pendants in both the Chapel of St Gregory and St Augustine and that of the Holy Souls are virtually identical and have been compared to Byzantine jewellery. From a frame of burnished bronze hang six shaded little lamps and droplets of semi-precious stone around a blue enamel medallion showing a dove. But most Byzantine of all must be the simple pierced bronze chandelier hanging in St Andrew's Chapel, with the clouds of heaven in gold mosaic above. Imagine olive oil and a burning taper in each of its nine glass beakers and you are back in the age of Justinian.

Just before his death Bentley wrote:

The westernmost dome is in strong light which streams through a large lunette window... The dome of the next is deeper in mysterious shadows; the third is still more so; while the sanctuary dome is brilliantly lighted by the twelve windows around its drum, so that our attention is led up to and powerfully focused upon the high altar.

As for Marshall, he was determined that his designs should be both true to the Byzantine tradition and up to Bentley's standards. The twin lines of great, gaunt chandeliers which march up the nave to the brilliantly lit sanctuary, and the delicate enamelled pendants to be seen hanging in the side chapels, form the basis on which his work on the Cathedral lighting can be judged.

The bronze chandelier in St. Andrew's Chapel with the Church of Santa Sophia
in Constantinople in the background

THE CATHEDRAL IN WARTIME

One of the questions often asked in the Cathedral is 'What happened in the war?' Visitors may see the blackened brickwork and have visions of the nave on fire from end to end with only a few valiant priests, nuns and choir boys left to stay the inferno. Disappointingly, nothing so spectacular occurred.

Of course, since the Cathedral was structurally complete in 1903 it witnessed two major wars. To an observer, probably the most obvious indication of the first, that of 1914-18, would have been the growing proportion of the congregation in uniform and the list of names of fallen Catholic servicemen going up in St George's Chapel. Air raids only became a regular occurrence fairly late in the war when the crypt, already in use by parishioners as a shelter, was officially inspected and approved for 2,000 people.

Throughout World War I the Choir School remained open and a regular morning occupation was the collection of shrapnel in the playground, which London Scottish soldiers were using to practise trench digging – creating an ideal battlefield for the boys. During the height of one air raid the boys are recorded as playing a game called 'buzz-one' in the Song School, 'buzzing out' being their sole concern, despite the noise of the bombs and guns outside.

Clearly the threat of air raids was much greater in 1939 and the Choir School was evacuated at the outset to Horsted Place, near Uckfield, reopening in 1946. During the war the Blessed Sacrament was exposed daily from 1-2pm but, because of the blackout, Christmas Midnight Mass and other evening Masses after sunset had to be suspended. An air raid post was set up at Archbishop's House, the crypt again brought into service as a shelter and it was arranged that Cathedral priests would go to local first-aid posts and casualty clearing stations in the event of serious air raids.

Fortunately, there was a breathing space from the declaration of war to the arrival of the bombers over London a year later. Inside the Cathedral the sanctuary columns were buttressed with protective scaffolding and sandbags to resist bomb blasts. The reliquary of St John Southworth was also heavily sandbagged. Meanwhile the clergy and lay staff formed fire-fighting parties, though initially equipped only with stirrup pumps and buckets.

In September 1940 the nightly blitz began. In October a small bomb hit the Choir School playground only 10 yards from the Choir School itself, creating a 30ft-deep crater. Fortunately, the soft clay absorbed the shock and nearby windows were not even cracked. Bricks, garden refuse and finally soil were thrown into the crater and in the space of nine months the chief sacristan had created an allotment garden surrounded by flower beds. It produced an annual crop of 130lb of vegetables and was featured both by the BBC and on Movietone News in the *Grow More Food* campaign.

In the same month, October 1940, Clergy House was hit, but only by a slab of concrete sent flying by a bomb in Vincent Square. In December it was hit again, this time by an unexploded anti-aircraft shell which did considerable damage to external brick and stonework before ending up in one of the priest's rooms. Within a short time many neighbouring buildings had been hit. St Andrew's Anglican church in Ashley Place, only 50 yards from the front of the

Cathedral, was damaged so badly it had to be pulled down, an explosion in Ashley Gardens shattered windows and woodwork in Archbishop's House and Cathedral Hall, and a delayed-action bomb fell near Morpeth Terrace. The following year, in May 1941, a flat in Ambrosden Avenue was destroyed, breaking many of the large leaded windows in the Cathedral sanctuary and nave, smashing doors and covering the Cathedral with debris.

The great domes of the Cathedral are covered with two layers of concrete, separated by concrete ribs which provide an air-space of some 3in between them. Even before the war the joints between the slabs of the outer domes had started to leak. The air-space between the two coverings provided perfect conditions for further damage from the blast and concussion of bombs exploding nearby. Slippage of the slabs allowed water to seep through both inner and outer casings, staining the interior white – as can still be seen today. It was only in the autumn of 1948 that all four domes were covered with copper sheeting, now an attractive feature of the Cathedral, partly paid for by the War Damage Commission.

It is remarkable that such a large building, covering four acres and close to obvious targets such as government buildings and Victoria Station, escaped almost unscathed. In part this is due to J F Bentley who, perhaps remembering the destruction by fire of his own parish church in Doncaster when he was a boy, built the Cathedral of largely fire-resistant materials. As a result, although one incendiary bomb burnt a large hole in the wood-block flooring of the Cathedral Hall and another went through the roof of the Choir School gymnasium, most tended to splatter and burn harmlessly on the concrete and asphalt of the Cathedral roof. Praise is also due to the efficiency of the fire fighters, eventually equipped with a motor trailer pump and a 50,000 gallon static water tank in the Choir School playground.

But the real reason why the Cathedral survived the war almost undamaged, when buildings all around were being hit, may lie elsewhere. One of the Daughters of Charity of St Vincent de Paul (the sisters who run the Passage Day Centre in Carlisle Place) installed a statue of Our Lady on the roof to protect them from air raids. During the 'Great Fire of London' of 1940 a lady watching the blaze at a flat next door saw something like a great hand keeping back the flames from the Carlisle Place community. It seems to have been protecting the Cathedral as well.

Wartime fireguard breaks for a Woodbine on the Cathedral roof

FROM DARKNESS TO LIGHT
THE UNKNOWN ARCHITECT

While the name of John Francis Bentley is almost synonymous with that of Westminster Cathedral, the name of John Marshall is known to few. In fact, Bentley only worked on the building from 1895 until his death in 1902. As his chief assistant, Marshall worked closely with him for these years and was subsequently responsible, over the next 25 years, for bringing to fruition many of Bentley's plans, which the architect had left unexecuted, and many of his own. It is Marshall whom we must thank for much that we see in the Cathedral today.

When Bentley died, on 2 March 1902, the structure of the Cathedral was essentially complete except for the top 50ft of the tower. But he had made no provision for carrying on the work after his death and it was Marshall, who had been his assistant over the preceding 25 years, who took on that responsibility. Quietly and conscientiously, Marshall set about establishing the firm of John F. Bentley, Son and Marshall, with himself as a partner. It was intended that Osmund Bentley, the architect's second son, would join the firm as soon as he had enough experience, but although Osmund did some work on the Cathedral, he subsequently lost interest in architecture.

The success of the Cathedral results in no small part from the fact that Marshall knew what Bentley intended and remained absolutely faithful to his vision. Thus the baldacchino, which was unveiled on Christmas Eve 1906 and which Bentley had described as the 'best thing about the Cathedral', is exactly according to Bentley's drawings, although the blue and gold patterned mosaic lining, which blends in perfectly, is of Marshall's design. Then the lighting, for which Bentley had left no plans, combines the style of Byzantine oil lamps with Bentley's designs for lighting elsewhere. The little pendants in the Chapel of the Holy Souls and that of St Gregory and St Augustine, for example, are remarkably similar to those in Bentley's Church of the Holy Rood, Watford.

Bentley had left drawings for the marblework in the Blessed Sacrament Chapel. But it was Marshall who designed the carved wooden canopy above the altar, the silver gilt tabernacle and all the other metalwork, including the extensive bronze gilt screens around the chapel, completed in 1907. Other metalwork designed by him can be seen in the 12 lovely bronze consecration sconces, each one in the shape of an arm bearing a candle, put up on 1 July each year in the nave to commemorate the dedication of the Cathedral. Marshall's versatility was also demonstrated in his plan for a pulpit. Realizing that the original marble pulpit, designed and made in Rome, was both unsuitable and increasingly insecure, his 'temporary' wooden pulpit, erected in 1914 in the position occupied by the present one, was used for 20 years. Another example of Marshall's work is the painted decoration of the Cathedral Hall – now restored to his original design.

Both in the Shrine of the Sacred Heart, and nearby, in the Vaughan Chantry, all the work, including the simple but effective red, green and gold mosaics in the barrel-roofed shrine, and Cardinal Vaughan's effigy and (empty) sarcophagus carved in white Pentelic marble for the chantry, are also to Marshall's designs. Similarly, although Bentley had prepared preliminary, partly coloured, designs for the marblework in St Paul's and St Joseph's Chapels, the detailed work fell to Marshall. During World War I, traditional Greek and Turkish marbles – verde antico, grey Hymettian, white Pentelic and streaked Proconnesian from the Island of Marmara – went up in St Paul's, the work in St Joseph's (the apse) being carried out in 1914.

Another reason for remembering Marshall is for his choice of others – the Nonconformist painter Robert Anning Bell RA, who designed both the lovely blue altarpiece in the Lady Chapel (1912) and the great tympanum mosaic over the main entrance doors (1916), and Eric Gill, the controversial sculptor who carved the Stations of the Cross during World War I. In both cases Marshall, a Nonconformist himself, faced opposition from Cardinal Bourne, who distrusted non-Catholics and was disappointed with both the blue altarpiece and the tympanum mosaic, describing it as 'the greatest disappointment I have received in connection with the work of the Cathedral'. As to the Stations, Gill, a Catholic convert from 1913, hints in his autobiography that it was only the bother of replacing them which prevented Bourne taking them down.

Marshall's later work included the marble and mosaics (by Anning Bell) in the apse (1922), the great marble organ screen above the narthex at the other end of the Cathedral (1924), and the Lady Chapel aisle and transept (1926). Perhaps his last project was designing the two bronze gilt angels, each bearing a trumpet, for the organ screen. They were installed on 23 December 1926. A little over a week later, on 1 January 1927, Marshall was dead. He was 75. Although he had completed other projects which Bentley had left unfinished – marble and mosaic work in the Church of Our Lady of the Assumption, Warwick Street, additional accommodation for St Thomas's Seminary, and a wooden altar for St John's Anglican church (both in Hammersmith) – the last 30 years of his life had centred on Westminster Cathedral.

A quiet and self-effacing man, Marshall was known to few outside his own family circle and immediate friends and colleagues. He was content to give all the credit for the Cathedral to Bentley and walk in his shadow. His intimate knowledge of Bentley's ideas, the structural problems presented by the building and how these were solved, is shown in a paper read by him to the Architectural Association in 1907. Unfailingly courteous, he refused to respond to often ill-conceived, and sometimes deliberately offensive, criticism of the Cathedral and its decoration. He has no memorial there, but just as Bentley's memorial is the Cathedral itself, so Marshall's consists of much of the decoration, including two bronze angels bearing trumpets.

SALVE ET VALE

Most people enter the Cathedral at the west end, with its impressive arch and mosaic surmounting three entrances, each with its own porch. On passing through one of these you are in the narthex, or anteroom, of the Cathedral, a place of arrivals and departures, of greetings and farewells. Ahead lie the nave and sanctuary, their division marked by the great hanging crucifix or rood.

The usual entry is through one of the side porches and here you are introduced to the Cathedral marbles – white Pentelic from near Athens, dark green verde antico and wavy green cipollino, both also from Greece, together with great slabs of purple and white breccia violetta from Tuscany. Each side porch contains a plinth of speckled green vert d'Estours marble from the French Pyrenees, inset with a violetta panel. These were designed by J F Bentley for the Church of Our Lady of the Assumption, Warwick Street (near Piccadilly), but transferred here in 1963.

The narthex is traditionally the place for waiting, where catechumens remained until they were baptized as Christians and where penitents awaited reintegration into the Christian community. Facing the left porch is the main holy water stoup in Hopton Wood stone from Derbyshire. The words inscribed above in Latin may be translated as 'Sprinkle me, Lord, with hyssop and I shall be cleansed; wash me and I shall be whiter than snow.' Making the sign of the cross with holy water on entering and leaving a church is, of course, a reminder of our own Christian baptism.

On the other side of the pier is a bronze statue of St Peter, a copy of that in St Peter's Basilica in Rome, erected in memory of the Reverend Luke Rivington. Inscribed on the side of the statue is 'A Röhrich, Roma' – the name of the artist responsible in Rome. The statue arrived from Rome in 1902 and was initially placed in St Peter's Crypt, before being judged too large for this position and moved upstairs to the narthex. The plinth is inscribed with a Latin inscription taken from St Matthew's Gospel (16:18). In translation this reads: 'You are Peter and upon this rock I will build my church.' In the same chapter Our Lord promises to give St Peter the keys of the Kingdom of Heaven. As a result keys are the symbol borne by St Peter and a useful way of identifying him in art. Here, as in Rome, his right foot is highly polished, resulting from the Catholic tradition of kissing or touching St Peter's foot and so showing allegiance to the first pope, the Bishop of Rome.

On the other side of the narthex from St Peter is the information desk and behind it the much-loved statue of St Anthony of Padua, hewn from a tree trunk and surrounded by candles. St Anthony was a Franciscan and is the patron saint of those searching for something (or someone) lost. The story behind this is that a novice once ran off with St Anthony's Psalter. As a result of his prayers the novice was visited by a terrifying apparition and so frightened by it that he returned the Psalter. St Anthony is known as 'the wonder worker'.

Above the narthex is the organ gallery with its great Henry Willis III organ, installed from 1922-32. It is linked electronically to the T C Lewis organ in the apse (1915), so the organist can play both at the same time. Because the

Cathedral is in the Byzantine style the organ pipes are concealed from the public view by a lattice of carved oak and, above the narthex, with a great marble screen with two bronze gilt angel musicians. The screen is supported by twin red granite columns with carved white Carrara capitals and black bases of Norwegian Larvikite. These columns are a reminder of the Precious Blood of Our Lord, to which the Cathedral is dedicated. From the arch between them, appropriately enough in a place where people wait, is the Cathedral clock.

The clock was designed by John Marshall, at that time head of the firm of Bentley, Son and Marshall. It was one of the last projects he undertook before his death on New Year's Day 1927. The clock was made in 1924 by Messrs Dent and Co of Cockspur Street, Trafalgar Square. Dents were chronometer, watch and clock makers to King George V, the Queen and the Prince of Wales. They were also primary standard timekeepers at the Royal Observatory, Greenwich, and made the 'Great Clock of the Houses of Parliament' – more generally known as Big Ben.

The Cathedral clock is made of mahogany, painted and gilded, and decorated with six scallop shells (the symbol of both St James and of pilgrims) with a winged hourglass below. It was paid for by a single donor, Mr E M Barker, and cost £264 – about £9,000 today. The bell above the casing originally rang each hour with a single note on the half hour – thus reminding both worshippers and clergy of the time. This mechanism was subsequently disconnected. On the afternoon of 24 September 1924 the clock was slowly raised into position using a light rope and tackle. But suddenly one of the ropes snapped under the strain and the clock crashed to the ground. Fortunately, there were no injuries but, although the glass face was not even cracked, the mechanism was badly damaged. After repair by Messrs Dent it was again raised to its present position (this time using a stronger rope) in February 1925.

It was initially expected that the proximity of the main doors and the vibration of the grand organ directly above would cause problems with the time-keeping. But after a month it was reported that the new clock was deviating by only 20 seconds a week. Sadly the blitz and more than 75 years' constant use have taken their toll and the clock is now considerably less reliable than it used to be. But then for many people, perhaps most, knowing the exact time somehow seems less important here in the quiet vastness of the Cathedral, than in the noisy and frenetic world outside.

Nave during construction looking east (note St Peter's statue)

THE START OF THE JOURNEY

The logical place to start a tour of the Cathedral chapels is in the Baptistry with its great marble font. This is where Cardinal Vaughan believed that such a tour should start, with the theme of baptism, finishing in the Holy Souls Chapel with those of death and judgement.

There are two entrances to the Baptistry. The first is from the right of the narthex, through bronze gilt gates dating from 1925. More impressive is the entrance from the Chapel of St Gregory and St Augustine. Between this chapel and the Baptistry is an impressive marble screen designed by J F Bentley and made by the marble merchants Whiteheads in 1902. Twin columns of cream-coloured pavonazzo marble stand between bronze gilt gates and grilles, supporting an arch and side panels inset with coloured marbles from the French Pyrenees. Approaching the Baptistry in this way one passes beneath an upper arch decorated with mosaics. Completed in 1904, they portray St John the Baptist and St Augustine, with representations of the waters of baptism on either side and the rivers of Paradise – Tigris, Phison, Gehon and Euphrates – in the soffit of the arch. The entrance thus unites the two chapels with their themes of baptism and conversion.

The central feature of the Baptistry is, of course, the great font, designed by Bentley. Octagonal and with an external diameter of 7ft 6in (5ft internally), it contains an impressive amount of water when filled, as it is prior to being blessed at the Easter vigil each year. Its size is a reminder of the early Christian practice of partial or total immersion. Indeed this still takes place, not only in the Baptist Church but also in Catholic churches such as that of St Charles Borromeo, Ogle Street, which has a font below floor level. A much smaller basin of water is at the side of the font in the Cathedral and it is this that is used by the celebrant. The font, of Italian and Greek marble, was given by the Dowager Lady Loder and ordered from Rome by Cardinal Vaughan, arriving in 1901. Bentley saw samples of the marbles used but it was assembled in situ by Roman masons after his death.

The marble floor of the Baptistry was made by Farmer and Brindley in 1912. White statuary encloses yellow Siena from Tuscany, Greek rosso antico and Connemara green from Ireland. The statue of St John the Baptist is a copy of one by the Danish artist, Thorwaldsen. It was given by the Third Marquess of Bute and is made of block tin from his Cornish tin mines. For many years it stood above the covered entrance to St Vincent's Centre in Carlisle Place, but in 1998 it returned, to be replaced there by a statue of St Vincent de Paul. Another item made for the Baptistry was a double confessional of carved, fumed Austrian oak which stood in the recess opposite the narthex entrance. It was the intention that most chapels should have a similar double confessional with single ones against the nave piers. That from the Baptistry now stands beside the information desk with another in St Paul's Chapel. A single is in St George's Chapel with another against the pier outside.

In 1948 a small, marble-clad altar was consecrated as a memorial to the Canadian Catholic airmen killed in the war.

Completed by Fennings in 1947, it stood in the recess below the Baptistry windows. Some 20 years later in 1966, designs were drawn up to complete the Baptistry decoration with marble and mosaics. Douglas Purnell, a painter and designer of stained glass, produced designs for the marblework and an Italian artist, Avenali, those for the mosaics. In the event the Advisory Art Committee of the Cathedral could not agree on the latter. The marble cladding of the walls took place in 1969, funded by a bequest from two of Bentley's daughters – Mrs Winefride de l'Hôpital and Miss H M Bentley. The memorial altar was replaced with plain white marble, the ceiling above the marble wall cladding white-washed and a new memorial to the Canadian Air Force erected near the main confessionals in the Lady Chapel transept in 1972.

Entering the Baptistry from the narthex, one passes a small wooden statue of St Christopher. It was given by the poet Hilaire Belloc for the protection of troops crossing the Channel, after seeing his eldest son leave for Flanders during World War I. St Christopher, of course, is the patron saint of travellers and thus perhaps an appropriate figure to pass on one's way to baptism and the start of another journey.

The Baptistry screen after erection in 1902 with St Gregory's Chapel beyond

SHAMROCKS AND SNAKES

Many who come to Westminster Cathedral were born in Ireland or have Irish ancestors. As a result the Chapel of St Patrick and the Saints of Ireland is one of the best known and loved. This is the Irish chapel in the Cathedral and symbols of Ireland and its saints appear everywhere.

Over 30 different types of marble have been used in the decoration, more than in any other chapel, and wherever possible Irish marbles have been used. Three of these appear in the altar, completed in 1910 and designed by John Marshall. The altar top and rectangular panel above it are of Irish black fossil marble from Kilkenny, the shamrocks in the panel being mother-of-pearl. The altar frontal is of wavy green Connemara from near Clifden in Galway, with centre and side panels of mushroom-coloured cipollino from Piedmont in Italy. The deep red panel in the middle is Victoria red, better known as Cork red, from a quarry near Midleton not far from Cork city.

As part of a tour children are sometimes asked to count the many shamrocks to be seen here. The shamrock was the 'visual aid' used by St Patrick in the fifth century to explain the Holy Trinity to the Irish. Children can also count the snakes (not forgetting to look at the top of the columns below the windows), which symbolize evil or the spiritual enemies of Christ. Curiously the elder Pliny, writing three centuries before St Patrick, states that no snake will touch a shamrock. Tradition has it that St Patrick expelled the snakes from Ireland but one refused. The saint therefore made a box and invited it to get in. The snake insisted that it was far too small to be comfortable and, after an argument, got in to prove it. Thereupon St Patrick slammed the lid and threw the box into the Irish Sea. The waves of the sea thus result from the writhings of the snake trying to get out. So ferry passengers suffering a bad passage should really blame St Patrick.

More Irish symbols, the shamrock of St Patrick and the oak leaf of St Bridget, appear in the pierced screen of white Carrara marble dividing the chapel from the nave. It is based on one in the Chiesa Metropolitana in Ravenna and was designed by Lawrence Shattock, then acting Cathedral architect, in 1928. The firm that made it, Farmer and Brindley, failed in 1929 after undertaking virtually all the marblework in the chapel. Apparently as a result of falling standards, mistakes were made in carving the screen that year and the work had to be done again in 1930. On the floor are more great slabs of Connemara green from near Clifden, together with smaller ones of mottled Cork red. In the centre is a large Celtic cross, so large you can easily overlook it. There are other Celtic motifs on the floor – in the corners and halfway down each side.

High on the west wall facing the altar are framed panels of ancient purple porphyry from Egypt, together with green smaragdite from Corsica – originally intended for a Corsican convent but found too hard to use. They are set in green and white vert d'Estours from the French Pyrenees. This also appears on the floor and looks a bit like peppermint. The south wall under the windows has 14 little columns of Cork red, each topped by a capital carved with snakes, doves and rams' heads. Between them are the badges of the Irish regiments which fought in World War I. With Irish independence in 1922, almost all these regiments were amalgamated or disbanded. Only the Irish Guards still remain, and for many years from 1950 the old colours of its 1st Battalion were laid up in St Patrick's Chapel while the Guards Chapel at Wellington Barracks was rebuilt following extensive damage from a flying bomb in 1944.

The only badge which is not of a regiment is that of the Royal Irish Constabulary, to the left of the windows. This force was succeeded by the Garda Siochana in the Republic and the Royal Ulster Constabulary in the North. On the other side of the altar, and originally planned for the opposite end of the chapel, is a cabinet of green verde antico marble. Inside is a book for each Irish regiment, recording those who died in World War I, together with another listing those killed while serving with other regiments – some 50,000 names in all.

With the marblework finished, in 1937 Boris Anrep was asked to design mosaics for the chapel. In 1914 he had designed angels for the vault of the inner crypt, close to Cardinal Manning's tomb, and in 1924 the mosaic of St Oliver Plunket, Archbishop of Armagh, martyred in 1681. That mosaic is in the aisle between St Patrick's and St Gregory's chapels. But Anrep's estimate for the mosaics in St Patrick's was beyond the Cathedral's means. The central feature of the chapel, the bronze gilt statue of St Patrick, dates from 1961 and was designed by Arthur Pollen. It replaced a framed picture of the saint. The marble reredos behind the statue was remodelled at the same time. The most recent work is the mosaic of St Patrick between the chapel and the aisle. It was produced by Trevor Caley and unveiled in March 1999. Appropriately the prevailing colour is green, St Patrick holds a shamrock and a snake writhes below.

It seems appropriate that St Patrick, a British boy taken as a slave to Ireland, who later returned there to become its spiritual leader and patron saint, should be remembered in this, the greatest of all Britain's Catholic cathedrals, where the roots of so many lie in Ireland.

St Patrick's Chapel in 1960, with the framed picture of St Patrick above the altar

CONTEMPLATION, SORROW AND PRAYER

What type of Stations of the Cross do you select for a great cathedral built in the Byzantine style, when Byzantine churches have no Stations of the Cross and the cathedral architect has died without leaving clear instructions? That was the problem facing the Westminster Cathedral authorities when the building was finished in 1903. The decision finally reached was deeply controversial but thought today to have been inspired.

Devotion to the Passion of Christ only became widespread from the twelfth and thirteenth centuries, fostered both by Crusaders returning from the Holy Land and by Franciscans, who took over responsibility for the holy places there in 1342. It was in Franciscan churches that devotion to the Way of the Cross, made up of a series of 'stops' or 'stations' first became commonplace, though the form of devotion could vary greatly and the number of stops could range from five to 30 or more. Only in 1731 did Pope Clement XII settle on the form of devotion to be followed and approve the custom of having 14 Stations of the Cross.

J F Bentley died in March 1902 without leaving designs for the Stations. But members of his family and colleagues at his firm were sure that he envisaged them in *opus sectile* – painted glass, cut and assembled to form patterns or pictures. Examples of the technique can be seen either side of the entrance to the Chapel of St Gregory and St Augustine in the Cathedral and Bentley used it in many churches elsewhere – as on the main altar frontal in St James, Spanish Place. The only Stations that Bentley is known to have designed are in the Church of the Sacred Heart in Wimbledon. But this is a Gothic-style church and Bentley's designs there are painted on canvas.

After Bentley's death his assistant for 25 years, J A Marshall, took over as architect in charge of the Cathedral. Drawings from this time show that *opus sectile* remained the plan for the Stations. A freelance artist, George Daniels, was asked to produce designs, five of which (undated) are still held. They show a marked resemblance to Bentley's designs in the Church of the Sacred Heart, Wimbledon, and in the case of the Fourteenth Station they are virtually identical. Clearly the intention at this time was to remain faithful to Bentley's vision.

Similarly, when the *Westminster Cathedral Chronicle* of March 1909 appealed for donors for the Stations, they were described as panels of *opus sectile* surrounded by white marble frames. By October all 14 had been paid for, the cost of each ranging from £62 initially to £75.11s at the end. In this way some £1,000 was raised and it was stated that 'The work will be put in hand at once'. The marble frames were in place by March 1910 but they were to remain empty for four years and were then taken down.

Not until October 1913 did the *Westminster Cathedral Chronicle* return to the subject, recording that cartoons of the Stations of the Cross, all but two by different artists, had been put up in the Cathedral for selection and approval which, 'with such a large number, should not be difficult'. A subsequent letter to the *Observer* suggested that Robert Anning Bell, a Nonconformist whose blue altarpiece went up in the Lady Chapel in late 1912, was 'within an ace of obtaining the Stations'. However, Cardinal Bourne, though growing increasingly restive at the absence of the Stations of the Cross in his ten-year-old Cathedral, did not like the altarpiece.

One of those asked to submit designs was Eric Gill. Only 31 and a sculptor for just three years, Gill met Marshall in August 1913 and set to work on preliminary drawings for 14 5ft 8in square stone carvings in low relief. The following April he presented the completed designs to Marshall and a week later was given the commission, Cardinal Bourne approving the agreement. Gill was delighted, writing 'I really was the boy for the job'. He set to work at once, using himself as a model in a mirror for the Tenth Station in which Jesus is stripped of His garments. Then followed the Second (Jesus receives the Cross), the Thirteenth (Jesus is taken down from the Cross) and the First (Jesus is condemned to death).

The first four Stations, including two of the best (the First and Thirteenth) were up by June 1915. It was then that, first in the *Universe* and then in the *Observer*, there appeared a series of critical letters, some abusive and most hostile. More reasoned was an article by P. G. Konody, the *Observer's* art critic. He accused Gill of assuming a 'child-like naiveté, a disguise of archaistic affectation' and of producing carvings utterly inexpressive of the sublime tragedy which they professed to portray. He added that Gill's relief carving was out of place in a Byzantine church and was never intended by Bentley, whose intentions regarding *opus sectile* had been deliberately disregarded.

Gill was interviewed in the *Observer* in October 1915. On the question of style he responded that he was simply a stone carver. 'I can only work in one style and that is my own.' He accepted that Bentley's intention was for *opus sectile* but this 'is factory work and to any real craftsmanship it is death'. It had been decided that it was not suitable for the Stations in the Cathedral and that they should be carved in low relief, which was the only form of carving used in a Byzantine building. As to the question why he had been given the commission he replied: 'I suppose that the architect approved of my work.'

So why did Gill get the job? Firstly he had been received into the Catholic Church in February 1913, and Cardinal Bourne wanted a Catholic. Secondly it seems to have been Marshall who decided on carved stone for the Stations, and who chose Gill, who had the technical ability to carve them. Marshall was a Nonconformist and Gill's restrained, unpretentious style clearly appealed to him. It should also be said that the drawings presented by Gill in the spring of 1914, on the basis of which he was chosen, are gentler and more expressive than the subsequent stone reliefs, which Gill seems to suggest in his autobiography would probably have been rejected by Bourne had he known. Last, and not least, Gill's fee was £765, considerably less than both the sum raised in 1909 and that asked for by 'posh' artists.

Gill's 1914 drawings show Latin biblical texts in three of the scenes. But Gill loved letters and finally included texts in nine of the Fourteen Stations – perhaps a pity as few now understand Latin and the decision after Gill's death in 1940 to colour the lettering red and black has made some scenes rather cluttered. Nevertheless, the series as a whole, designed to be seen with the figures thrown into relief by light coming in from the side, have many attractive and unusual features – the boys Alexander and Rufus following their father in the Fifth, the dice with the two and one uppermost

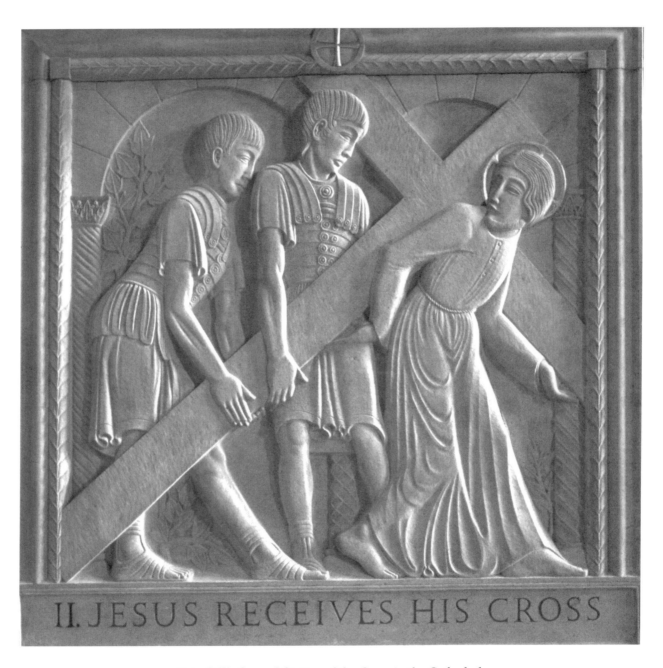

II. JESUS RECEIVES HIS CROSS

Eric Gill's Second Station of the Cross in the Cathedral

(the Holy Trinity?) in the Tenth, the wound in Jesus's left side (by tradition and in Gill's 1914 drawings on the right), and Jesus blessing even in death in the Twelfth and Fourteenth.

So what of the Stations today? They were first used on Good Friday 1918 and Gill explained them in the *Westminster Cathedral Chronicle*. A deeply committed Catholic, for Gill the Stations were both a statement of personal belief and church furniture carved for his fellow Catholics, as a focus for prayer. Thus he has portrayed only those referred to in the Gospels, and these impassively. As to the crowd along the Jerusalem road, we are that crowd. Contemplation, sorrow and prayer must come from within ourselves – those who still follow the Way of the Cross to Calvary, especially during Lent and Holy Week, those who still watch along the Way.

THE THREE PULPITS

There is something in the Cathedral which at its first appearance was squat, fat and a bit out of place, served for only 11 years before hibernating for a further 20, re-emerged twice its original size to serve triumphantly for 30 years but has now been in semi-retirement for almost 40. It is, in fact, the pulpit.

The first tentative plans for the Cathedral, produced in 1895 by J F Bentley, show the pulpit on the left of the nave – first of all in the north-east corner, close to where the lectern is now used at Mass, and then against the pier at the north-west corner of the north transept, directly across the nave from the present pulpit. But in 1896 Bentley's drawings show that he had adopted a position on the right-hand side of the nave, exactly where the present pulpit stands today.

The first pulpit was ordered in Rome by Cardinal Vaughan in 1902 and was installed in the Cathedral the following year. It was designed and produced by Cavaliere Aristide Leonori, an artist employed by the Vatican who had never seen Westminster Cathedral and admitted the unsuitability of his design when he eventually did. Bentley had died in early 1902 and had nothing to do with the pulpit, which was paid for by Ernest Kennedy, an important benefactor of the Cathedral.

The first pulpit was large enough to accommodate the archbishop and two assistants (his master of ceremonies and cross-bearer). It was not where the present pulpit is situated, which is where Bentley had planned it, but one bay further forward – near the Thirteenth Station of the Cross. It was 11ft wide and 5ft deep and raised the preacher 4ft above floor level. It was made of marble inlaid with red and green porphyry and mosaic in the Cosmatesque style.

As the years went by criticism of the pulpit increased. Its inconvenient steps, position and small size (55ft square feet internally) were now being exacerbated by ominous creaking and shaking which could only be ignored by the most resolute of preachers. As early as 1905 John Marshall had proposed alterations. A replacement finally became essential and on Good Friday 1914 a temporary wooden pulpit, polygonal in plan and 9ft in diameter, was first used. It was erected one bay further back from the sanctuary than the original pulpit (which remained), and was thus where the present pulpit is. It provided an area of some 64 sq ft and was to be in use for 20 years.

In 1934 Cardinal Francis Bourne, Vaughan's successor, had served 30 years as Archbishop of Westminster and 50 as a priest. To commemorate both this and the restoration of the Shrine of Our Lady of Walsingham he donated a permanent pulpit. The wooden one was taken down but rather than starting afresh Bourne instructed Lawrence Shattock, the Cathedral architect, to reconstruct the first pulpit. Its lower panels were brought up and new columns made to bear the weight of the structure. In August 1934, on the Feast of the Assumption, the 'new pulpit' was blessed.

In this manner the lovely central panel of the Lamb of God, the figures of the evangelists, and almost all the Roman Cosmatesque panels were retained – one being used to decorate the wall behind the preacher. The original lower central panel was turned upside down and an inscription recording the reconstruction inserted. A new panel in *opus sectile* by

John Trinick, portraying Our Lady of Walsingham, was put in place to face the sanctuary. From the wooden pulpit only the sounding board was retained; this was subsequently discarded.

It was a masterly example of recycling; only the little spiral columns on the front of the first pulpit and some of its minor marble panels were unused. With the addition of eight new columns to support the structure, and pavonazzo and cipollino marble cladding for its new staircase, the 1934 pulpit was 14 ft wide and 7 ft deep. It thus provided the preacher and his assistants with an area of 100 sq ft, almost twice the size of the original, and raised them 5 ft 9 in above floor level.

Each of the columns supporting the 1934 pulpit, the one to be seen today, is surmounted by an attractive capital, including one with four peacocks. The last, that furthest from the sanctuary, bears the initials EK and FB – Ernest Kennedy and Francis Bourne who, though separated by three decades, together provided the pulpit. For more than 30 years it was in regular use. But with the changes brought about by the Second Vatican Council it is now employed only on great feast days and other special occasions, such as the annual Christmas celebration.

The original pulpit installed in 1903

OUR LADY OF WALSINGHAM AND THE MISSING GOSPELS

The Cathedral pulpit has on its side a representation of Our Lady of Walsingham. But if you look at this closely you will see that the Book of the Gospels held by the Holy Child in the statue at Walsingham is absent, and if you look more closely still you will notice that the seven rings on the uprights either side of Our Lady's high-backed throne, symbolizing the Seven Sacraments, have been reduced to four on the Cathedral pulpit.

It must be admitted that we do not know what the original statue of Our Lady at Walsingham looked like. The Priory of Augustinian Canons at Walsingham was established in 1153 and the wooden statue enshrined in the Holy House nearby seems to date from about this time. For 300 years Walsingham ranked with Jerusalem, Rome and Santiago de Compostela as one of the major shrines in Europe, and English kings from Henry III to Henry VIII were pilgrims and benefactors.

In 1511, the year of Henry VIII's pilgrimage, Erasmus also went there. He describes the statue as 'a small image, neither excelling in material nor workmanship but in virtue most efficacious'. Some 20 years later, on 18 September 1534, the Prior of Walsingham, Richard Vowel, together with his canons, acknowledged the Royal Supremacy and four years after this the statue was taken from the shrine and burned at Cromwell's house in Chelsea. The canons were pensioned off, the priory was destroyed and the Holy House, which contained the statue, was burned to the ground.

It is more than a little ironic that Henry VIII's resolve to exert his personal authority over the Church resulted in our best evidence for the appearance of Our Lady of Walsingham. For attached to the acknowledgement of Supremacy of 1534 was a clear impression of the thirteenth-century seal of Walsingham Priory. Now in the British Museum this is of white wax about 3in in diameter. On one side appears the Priory Church and on the other Our Lady with a lily-sceptre, enthroned in a high-backed throne adorned with seven rings. On her left knee is the Holy Child holding the Book of the Gospels.

The other evidence we have for the appearance of the statue at Walsingham is derived from pilgrim souvenir badges or tokens. With pilgrims to Walsingham travelling from far afield, these have been discovered in King's Lynn, London, Salisbury and elsewhere. A variety of different badges can be associated with Walsingham, some of them resembling the priory seal, but many other shrines to Our Lady existed in medieval England and since few tokens were inscribed, those from Walsingham are difficult to distinguish. In addition almost all were crudely moulded of lead, are usually damaged and show little detail.

It was not until the late nineteenth century that there was a resurgence of interest in Walsingham. By that time there was not a single Catholic living there. But in 1897 the parish Church of the Annunciation was built in King's Lynn, the centre and port for most medieval pilgrims visiting Walsingham. Included in the church was a chapel dedicated to our Lady of Walsingham, based on the thirteenth-century Holy House of Loreto in Italy and with a statue modelled on Our Lady of Cosmedin in Rome. Pope Leo XIII declared this to be the Shrine of Our Lady of Walsingham.

Meanwhile an Anglican, Charlotte Boyd, had bought the fourteenth century Slipper Chapel, the last of the wayside chapels on the pilgrim road to Walsingham. In 1894 she became a Catholic. But not long afterwards, in 1897, the shrine was declared to be at King's Lynn and her chapel remained unused. It was not until July 1933 that the newly-appointed Bishop Youens, whose Diocese of Northampton encompassed Walsingham, publicly pledged to restore the pilgrimage to Walsingham and set about restoring the Slipper Chapel as a shrine. Cardinal Bourne seized on the idea and announced that he would lead a National Pilgrimage there. And so, on 19 August 1934, the cardinal led 12,000 pilgrims back to Walsingham and the first Mass since the Reformation was held in the Slipper Chapel, the new National Shrine.

For the occasion Bishop Youens had commissioned Professor Tristram, a medieval historian, to design a new statue of Our Lady of Walsingham, the gift of Miss Hilda Carey of Cromer and Torre Abbey, Devonshire. Tristram accordingly made a drawing of the 1534 seal impression of Walsingham Priory and this was used to carve a small wooden statue of Our Lady, enthroned by Bishop Youens in the Slipper Chapel on 16 August 1934, three days before the National Pilgrimage. But it is clear from a photograph of Tristram's drawing, which appeared in the *Illustrated London News* at the time, that important details were omitted, notably the Book of the Gospels and the seventh ring symbolizing the sacraments. And so these were also omitted in the statue.

Meanwhile in Westminster Cathedral, Cardinal Bourne had instructed Lawrence Shattock to remodel the pulpit. John Trinick was commissioned to produce a new panel for it in *opus sectile* representing Our Lady of Walsingham. Although to be in the same style as the pulpit, this clearly needed to resemble the new statue at Walsingham. Indeed the blessing of the pulpit occurred only the day before that of the statue. Both Tristram's drawing and Trinick's initial design had been completed by March 1934 when the latter appeared in an exhibition of liturgical art. It seems clear that Trinick took his design from Tristram's drawing and so, like the 1934 statue, the Gospels were omitted and the seven rings were incomplete.

Twenty years afterwards, on the Feast of the Assumption in the Marian Year of 1954, the papal delegate crowned the statue in the Slipper Chapel. But it was not the 1934 statue based on Tristram's drawing. Recognizing that this lacked important details shown in the Walsingham Priory seal, a new statue was carved by Marcel Barbeau for the occasion and this is the one in the Slipper Chapel today. Our Lady's throne is adorned with the seven rings of the sacraments while the Holy Child holds a small book of the Gospels in his left hand in token of the Word made Flesh. So, even if we cannot be sure that the statue we see today is the same as that seen by medieval pilgrims, at least we know that it resembles Our Lady of Walsingham as shown on the seal of Walsingham Priory.

And, after all, an image is never really important. As those who go on pilgrimage to Walsingham will know, despite the destructive efforts of Henry VIII and Thomas Cromwell, despite the subsequent centuries of neglect, Walsingham lives on, Our Lady's shrine deep in the English countryside, a timeless and very peaceful place. For Our Lady is there.

OUR LADY OF WESTMINSTER

There is one statue in Westminster Cathedral which is far, far older than any of the others. It is also probably the most venerated. It is the medieval statue known as Our Lady of Westminster.

The flat-backed figure is enshrined below Eric Gill's Thirteenth Station of the Cross – in which the body of Jesus is returned to his Mother's arms. The figure is of alabaster and shows Our Lady enthroned and crowned with a broken sceptre in her left hand. Traces of paint indicate that Our Lady's crown, sceptre and mantle-fastening were gilded. Her garments were edged with gold with interior folds painted blue and red. Her dark brown throne stood amidst daisies in a dark green field.

The Holy Child's position on the right and the corded mantle fastening are characteristic of English alabaster figures made between about 1440 and 1525 but it is not yet possible to say with certainty where individual statues were made. Nottingham appears to have been the production and distribution centre for the alabaster industry from 1340 to 1550. With nearby quarries, particularly at Chellaston, 15 miles to the south-west, supplying the raw material, large numbers of altarpiece panels, plaques and statues were carved and painted there. Contemporary records also indicate that alabaster was carved at Chellaston, York, London, Burton-on-Trent and elsewhere.

The systematic destruction of religious images at the Reformation, particularly during the reign of Edward VI (1547-53), resulted in few surviving in England. Fortunately, English alabaster work was much in demand abroad, particularly in France, both before and during this period. Thus eight months after an Act for the destruction of images in England in January 1550, the English ambassador to France was reporting to the Privy Council the arrival of three or four ships from England laden with religious images to be sold in Paris, Rouen and elsewhere. Of the 40 or more English alabaster statues of the Virgin and Child now identified, the majority either are, or were, in France.

At least 12 of these figures, including Our Lady of Westminster, depict Our Lady seated with the Child on her right knee. Of these, five are now in France, three in England, two in Glasgow, one in Germany and one in Houston, Texas. Only one of these appears to have survived the Reformation in England. This was found buried behind the Church of All Saints at Broughton-in-Craven, Yorkshire, in 1863, but Our Lady's head and left arm are missing. The statue in the Cathedral, one in the British Museum and one in Glasgow, all appear to have been purchased in France in 1954-6. The figure now in the Museum of Fine Arts, Houston, was also purchased at this time by a French immigrant couple living in America.

Our Lady of Westminster, with a height of over 36 in, is one of the largest of the 12 seated figures. The smallest (16 in) is in other respects very similar and can be seen in the St Mungo Museum of Religious Life and Art in Glasgow. The Cathedral figure also bears a close resemblance to that found buried in the churchyard at Broughton-in-Craven which, at 30in, would be precisely the same height were the head still in place. It seems a real possibility that they were made in the same workshop – perhaps even by the same craftsman.

Before the Reformation, All Saints Church, Broughton-in-Craven, was dedicated first to St Oswald and then to St

Oswald and Our Lady. Originally Norman, the nave was enlarged in the fifteenth century and a chantry chapel built in the north-east corner in 1442. Chantry chapels in nearby churches were dedicated to Our Lady and this would account for the change of name at Broughton. A Lady Chapel would have needed a statue.

In 1863 two alabaster statues of the Virgin and Child were found buried in the ground at the rear of All Saints. One was of Our Lady seated with the Christ Child (with head and left arm missing) on the left. The style shows that it was made in the fourteenth century. The second dates from the fifteenth century and is remarkably similar to that in Westminster Cathedral. The Broughton statues were presumably defaced and buried at the Reformation. Statues, which were usually heavy, were quite often buried near the church from which they came.

The fourteenth-century figure would have been positioned in the nave or chancel. The roof of the chancel is also fourteenth century so the statue could have been acquired at the same time. It seems extremely probable that the fifteenth-century statue was acquired for the new Lady Chapel, built in 1442, and positioned above the altar. Alabaster figures were carved both for a specific customer and in quantity from a standard pattern. In either case the Broughton figure would date from the early 1440s. The statue in Westminster Cathedral, while very similar, is a little more ornate. It seems safe to say that it was made about 1450, most probably in Nottingham or nearby.

The statue now in Westminster Cathedral was first recorded in 1930 when it came up for sale in Paris. It reappeared in 1954 in an Exhibition des Chefs d'Oeuvre de la Curiosité du Monde at the Louvre, on loan from the Paris art dealers Brimo de Laroussilhe who state it was acquired from the Baron de Saint Leger Daguerre, living in Paris. The statue was then bought by an English ecclesiastical art dealer, S W Wolsey, in November 1954 and exhibited by him in June 1955 at the Antique Dealers' Fair in London. He subsequently displayed it at his premises at 71 Buckingham Gate, now replaced by a modern office block.

Cardinal Griffin, Archbishop of Westminster, wanted the statue for the Cathedral. But first to bid for it was the Dean of York Minster. An appeal by him for funds failed, however, despite a substantial donation by Sir William Milner. The dean then suggested that Westminster Cathedral should have it. In October 1955 it was announced that the sale had been completed. It was fitting that York Minster was represented by Milner at the Solemn Evening Mass on 8 December 1955, the Feast of the Immaculate Conception, with the Cathedral Choir welcoming the statue with the *Salve Regina*.

So how and where did the medieval alabaster – Our Lady of Westminster – survive the Reformation? Most probably the figure was exported to France soon after it was made, destined for a French church, abbey or shrine. The similarity with the Broughton figure might suggest that it was first made for the home market and only later sent to France to escape destruction. But there is no other evidence for this. During the French Revolution, when many shrines were destroyed or vandalized, it probably came into private hands.

Speculation will continue about the history of this serene and touching sculpture. Yet what really matters is that, 500 years after it was carved and coloured, a very rare and beautiful English pre-Reformation portrayal of the Virgin and Child has pride of place in a nineteenth-century cathedral – our own Lady of Westminster. *Salve Regina, Mater misericordiae; vita dulcedo, et spes nostra, Salve.*

A STILL POINT IN A TURNING WORLD

Some years ago a couple, who could not speak much English, approached the information desk in the Cathedral. They wanted to see the Spanish Chapel. The initial reaction was that they believed they were in Westminster Abbey, as many visitors do. But the Abbey does not have a Spanish Chapel. And then, quite suddenly, a distant memory returned.

Cardinal Vaughan came from an old-established recusant family. He was the eldest of 13 children. Eliza Vaughan, their mother, prayed for an hour each day before the Blessed Sacrament that her children should receive a religious vocation. The third son, Kenelm Vaughan, was only 13 when his mother died and he remained, like her, devoted to the Blessed Sacrament all his life. His elder brother, Herbert, was later to write of him that 'Kenelm impresses me more and more as a saint than anyone I know'.

So it was that 40 years later, in 1896, while Cardinal Vaughan was building Westminster Cathedral, his younger brother Kenelm, now also a priest, obtained permission from his superiors to raise funds for a chapel within it dedicated to the Blessed Sacrament. A fluent Spanish speaker, he travelled first to Spain which he already knew. There he spent two years raising almost £4,000 from subscribers who included King Alfonso XIII and the Queen Mother, Maria Christina. Contributors of £50 or more were entitled Fundadores del Sagrario (Founders of the Tabernacle). Years later, in 1905, King Alfonso came to pray in the Cathedral and chapel which he had helped to found.

From Spain, Father Kenelm travelled to South America, where he had also been before. Here, begging from door-to-door among the Spanish-speaking peoples of countries such as Argentina, Chile, Peru and Ecuador, he raised well over £14,000 in nine years. When he returned to England in 1907, four years after the opening of Westminster Cathedral and the death of its archbishop, his brother, he had raised a total of £18,634 (about £800,000 today). Two years later, on 19 May 1909, he died, his Solemn Requiem Mass being held in the Cathedral to which he had devoted so many years of his life.

With the money given so generously and wholeheartedly by the peoples of Spain and South America, who contributed as if to a project in their own countries, work on the Blessed Sacrament Chapel could start. In fact, J F Bentley had originally planned that the chapel would be to the right of the sanctuary, where the Lady Chapel now stands, with a baldacchino borne on six columns over the altar and tabernacle. But it was then realized that processions would need to pass this chapel on their way to and from the sanctuary, and all would need to genuflect before the Blessed Sacrament. The difficulties this might cause resulted in the chapel being positioned where it is today. Decoration started in 1904 and over the next four years the marblework, altar, carved wooden canopy and most of the gilded and enamelled metalwork were completed, leaving £3,750 unspent for the mosaics.

The entrance gates and screen around the chapel are of bronze gilt. They cost almost £4,000 and took three and a half years to make. They emphasize that this is a special chapel, the place where the Blessed Sacrament is reserved.

Within the silver gilt tabernacle is a steel safe containing the Consecrated Host. It is lined with Lebanon cedar and concealed by a white silk curtain suspended from 29 gold wedding rings, each inscribed with the name of its donor. The altar crucifix and candlesticks, primitive Byzantine in style, were the gift of another donor in 1909. Although Bentley had left designs for the marblework, all the metalwork and the wooden canopy, which Cardinal Vaughan had ruled should replace the planned baldacchino on grounds of cost, were designed by John Marshall, then architect in charge.

Almost 50 years and two world wars went by before any further work was done on the Blessed Sacrament Chapel. Then in 1956 Boris Anrep, a Russian by birth and already over 70, was commissioned to design mosaics for its completion. The little pieces of glass were made in Venice and there fixed to working drawings prior to being crated and finally put into place in the Cathedral from 1960 to 1962. The cost was £45,000 (about £500,000 today). In 1914 Anrep had designed mosaic angels for the vault near Cardinal Manning's tomb in the inner crypt, and ten years later he undertook the mosaic of St Oliver Plunket in the aisle near St Patrick's Chapel. He was one of the first modern mosaicists to design floors, perhaps his best being on the first-floor landing of the National Gallery.

Before the entrance gates of the Blessed Sacrament Chapel there is a niche on either side, one displaying a peacock – symbolizing immortality and the all-seeing eyes of God – and the other showing a phoenix – a symbol of the Resurrection. They were given by the Guild of the Blessed Sacrament. Above the entrance gates stand the Archangels Michael and Gabriel as celestial guards. The chapel mosaics illustrate the themes of the Trinity, sacrifice and the bread and wine of the Eucharist. On the inner side of the entrance arch appear Abraham and his wife entertaining three angels – a symbol of the Trinity. This is again represented in the next scene, where Shadrach, Meshach and Abednego are in the burning fiery furnace. Then a medallion contains the Lamb of God – Christ, of course – between two angels with censers.

On the left wall the theme is sacrifice, prefiguring that of Christ. Abel is shown as the first to make an acceptable offering to God. Next is Abraham, prepared to sacrifice his only son Isaac until stayed by the angel. Then Malachias, the last of the Prophets, appears with candlestick and censer, kneeling before the Angel of the Covenant. Finally Samuel, the last of the Judges, listens intently to the voice of the Lord, with a sacrificial knife abandoned before the altar. On the right the theme of sacrifice is repeated, with Noah and his family about to offer up a lamb after the Flood. Shem's basket contains a pair of hoopoes, representing the survival of all living things, but they look also as if they were much-loved ark pets. The scenes of the gathering of manna and Elias being urged by an angel to eat, point towards the Eucharist, while in the niches are Abraham and Melchisadek, the priest of God, who brought him bread and wine and blessed him after the battle.

The sanctuary arch bears 12 doves – representing the apostles. They mark the transition from the chapel nave, with its scenes from the Old Testament, to the sanctuary which is concerned with the New. On the left is the wedding feast at Cana and the Resurrection, on the right the feeding of the 5,000 and the liberation of captive souls. In the centre is the triumphant, jewelled Cross rising above the globe and the Church, represented by St Peter's Basilica in Rome. Its foundation is the rock from which flow the four rivers of Paradise. And high above, the Pantocrator, Christ in Glory, between the Hand of God and the Holy Spirit in the form of a dove – the Trinity.

The Blessed Sacrament Chapel is almost always occupied by people, not all of them Catholics, in silent thought and prayer. It is a place of private devotion where time seems to stand still, voices seem distant and where even children become quiet. A place where many find the peace for which they have been searching, a still point in a turning world.

CATHEDRAL MARBLES
THE MARBLE SEEKERS

It all started at the Paris Opéra. Then a young Italian in Algeria got into the act, and finally an Englishman decided to do the job properly. They were the marble seekers – men who, some 125 years ago, went searching for marble quarries, many of them used by the Romans and then abandoned and lost for 1,500 years. Without these men Westminster Cathedral would look very different.

The first was Charles Garnier, chosen from 171 contenders to be the architect of the new Paris Opera House which was opened, amidst great publicity, in 1875. The style he adopted was a new one, 'the style of Napoleon III' as he put it, and the materials used included many varieties of marble, particularly for the grand staircase. One of these, Swiss cipollino, was used there for the first time. Twin columns of it are now at the entrance of the Chapel of St Gregory and St Augustine in the Cathedral. Garnier wanted to revive the full-scale use of marble for decoration. But the material was largely available only in small amounts for mantelpieces, paving, table-tops and tombs. So Garnier went looking.

The marbles he eventually assembled came from Algeria, France, Italy, Scotland (granite), Spain, Sweden and Switzerland. Most, including black and white grand antique des Pyrenées and green Campan vert, are also in the Cathedral. Obtaining 30 great load-bearing columns for around the grand staircase was a particular problem. After looking at every possibility Garnier finally chose yellow Sarancolin from a quarry half-way up a high mountain in the Pyrenees. In January 1863 he went there to inspect the blocks. It was piercingly cold, there was deep snow and oxen had turned the paths into liquid mud. 'C'était horrible' wrote Garnier.

Meanwhile a penniless young Italian from the Del Monte family of marble merchants in Carrara had gone to Algeria soon after the French conquest. His first discovery was of Algerian onyx quarries near Tlemcen in 1849. At some risk to his life, for the countryside was unsubdued, he approached the local Arabs and bought the quarries for a small amount, subsequently selling them on. Then, in excavations near Arzeu, he discovered mosaics of a totally different marble, so he set out to find its source. What he eventually found in about 1875, high on a mountain plateau north-east of Oran, were the old Roman quarries of Kleber.

French geologists had surveyed the area for iron ore but not for marble; for iron, while not present commercially, had stained the porous rock red. From a natural creamy white on the eastern plateau the marbles ranged through rose to a red-flushed yellow. To the west, great earth movements had fragmented the rock and water had subsequently carried iron oxide into the fissures, staining the breccia from orange to a deep blood-red. Marbles from these quarries, which Del Monte immediately arranged to exploit, now decorate the walls of the Lady Chapel (pink-flushed giallo antico), those of the Blessed Sacrament Chapel (deep pink rose de Numidie), the altar frontal of St George's, the floor in the Holy Souls Chapel and the nave piers at gallery level (all brèche sanguine).

Back in England events were being closely watched by a young sculptor named William Brindley. Described by Sir George Gilbert Scott in 1873 as 'The best carver I have met with ... A man whose whole soul is absorbed and devoted to his art,' Brindley was the sculptor chosen by Scott for the capitals and other stonecarving on the Albert Memorial. In 1860 Brindley formed a partnership with another sculptor, William Farmer, at premises on Westminster Bridge Road. Initial commissions, many of them working to Scott's designs, consisted mainly of stone and wood carvings for churches but also included plaster models of animals, prior to their execution in terracotta, for the façade of the Natural History Museum, Kensington.

But by 1880, like Garnier and Del Monte before him, Brindley had decided that marble was a material of the future. Knowing from Garnier's 1878 book about the Opera House that he had failed to obtain Greek cipollino from Euboea (he used Swiss instead), Brindley went there and arranged to supply it. After previously listing themselves simply as sculptors, in 1881 Farmer and Brindley advertised as 'Sole agents for cipollino'. Columns of this wavy green marble are now at the entrance to the Chapels of St Joseph, St Patrick and St Paul and in the Cathedral transepts.

The year 1886 saw Brindley on the Greek island of Chios searching for the ancient quarries of africano marble. Instead he discovered those of porta santa. 'Pliny was wrong' he complained. The following year, determined to find the source of perhaps the most famous Roman marble, the purple porphyry of the emperors, he set off into the Egyptian Eastern Desert with 19 attendants and 15 camels. After a week in the saddle he found the porphyry blocks and quarries used at the time of Hadrian, at Gebel Dokhan, the Mountain of Smoke, 25 miles from the Red Sea. By this time, he wrote, the water from the goatskin 'tasted like hot, rancid, bacon broth'. The following year Farmer and Brindley's listing in the Trades Directory included the words 'Quarry proprietors of ancient Egyptian porphyry'.

Because of the isolation of the desert quarries and the great hardness of the stone, porphyry was not a commercial success, but Brindley's next venture was. Using a description by Paul the Silentiary (Emperor Justinian's court poet) at the opening of the Church of Santa Sophia, Constantinople, in 563, Brindley set off to find the source of the celebrated Roman marble, verde antico. After a quest which lasted from 1886-92, Brindley found ten ancient quarries near Larissa in Thessaly, Greece, and arranged to exploit them. Eight columns of this dark green marble, the first to be hewn for 1,300 years, now line the nave of the Cathedral, with three more at the transepts, while slabs of the lighter varieties appear in almost every chapel.

Meanwhile, orders for marble decoration were increasing as Brindley had foreseen. There was a building boom in England from 1897-1906 and again from 1910-14 and marble was fashionable. Major commissions completed by Farmer and Brindley included Surrey House, Norwich (1904), the Victoria and Albert Museum (1909) and the National Gallery (1911). Westminster Cathedral was a continuing source of work. The structural columns with their carved capitals (1900) were followed by the baldacchino (1906), the Blessed Sacrament Chapel (1907), Lady Chapel (1908), Sacred Heart Shrine, Vaughan Chantry and remaining altars (all 1910), Baptistry floor (1912), St Andrews Chapel (1915) and St Paul's (1917).

From 1908-23 Farmer and Brindley advertised as 'Largest establishment and with greatest variety and stock of

Some of the many different marbles installed by Farmer and Brindley in the sanctuary

choice coloured marbles and rare stones in the Kingdom'. But World War I resulted in a slump in demand. Brindley died in 1919 and without him the heart seemed to go out of the firm. London's County Hall and Glasgow's City Council Chambers provided work until 1922-3 but commissions elsewhere were sparse. In Westminster Cathedral the apse wall was decorated in 1921 and the organ screen in 1924, while intermittent work on St Patrick's Chapel took place from 1923-9. Here went some of Brindley's rarest remaining marbles – framed panels of purple porphyry, dark green brèche universelle from the Nile and lighter green smaragdite from Corsica on the west wall, with costly lapis lazuli and diamonds of grey africano set in red Languedoc over the niches beside the altar.

In 1929 Farmer and Brindley appeared in the Trades Directory simply as marble decorators. In the same year the firm ceased trading. For many years the site on Westminster Bridge Road lay derelict. It is now a block of flats. Besides being a talented sculptor and businessman, William Brindley was a traveller and adventurer. Without the marbles which he found and his firm installed, without Del Monte's discoveries in Algeria and without Garnier's determination to revive the use of marble in a building of which France could be proud, the Cathedral would be the poorer.

CIPOLLINO

Marbles and onions are not usually associated, but the Italian for onion is 'cipolla' and cipollino marble received its name because of its resemblance to a cut onion. Greek cipollino is believed to have been one of the first coloured marbles brought to Rome and it was the one most used. In Westminster Cathedral it can be seen cladding walls and piers in the nave, lining the wall of the apse and in virtually every chapel.

Cipollino has become a term for marble banded with different shades of green, white and yellow. Thus besides Greek cipollino, the Cathedral also has columns of the waxy yellow Swiss cipollino (from Saillon in the Canton Valais) at the entrance to St Gregory's, St Andrew's and St George's Chapels. The green veined but more putty coloured Italian cipollino alternates with the darker Connemara green marble behind the altar on the wall of St Patrick's. But these have been used for perhaps 200 years whereas that from Greece has been used for over 2,000.

Greek cipollino was worked first by the Greeks and then by the Romans. Pieces for mosaic floors were brought to Rome as early as the second century BC. But it was in Julius Caesar's time, about 48 BC, that solid columns and wall panels from Carystus were first recorded as being used for a private house. Carystus (Karystos) is on the south-west coast of the Greek island of Euboea (Evia) and the Romans named the marble Marmor Carystium. The quarries were worked extensively as imperial property until Byzantine times, the 'fresh green of Carystus' being used in Justinian's Church of Santa Sophia in Constantinople, opened in 563.

Today cipollino can be found throughout the old Roman Empire. There are over 500 columns in Rome itself. The Temple of Antoninus and Faustina in the Roman Forum has ten columns of the marble 36 ft in height. Slabs can seen on shop counters in Pompeii and Herculaneum and all across Italy and Greece, as well as in Roman outposts such as Carthage. Recycled Roman cipollino can also be found in many Christian churches. There are eight columns of it in the portico of St Peter's in Rome, and St Mark's in Venice has smaller columns beside one of the entrances with slabs of it on the interior walls and floor.

For 1,300 years the old quarries lay forgotten. But in the 1860s Charles Garnier wrote to Greece for cipollino for the new Grand Opera House of Paris (opened in 1875). He was told that the quarries were abandoned and the cost would be prohibitive. So Garnier was the first to use the recently discovered Swiss cipollino instead. He described the incident in his book on the Opera House in 1878 and it appears to have been this which motivated William Brindley to travel to Euboea to search out and reopen the ancient quarries there.

Brindley's search lasted several years. It culminated in the discovery of workable marble in a series of old Roman quarries on the side of Mount Pyrgari, near Styra. Some 13 miles to the south-east and 3 miles north-east of Karystos, he found Kylindroi quarry where ten ancient columns still lie half-way up Mount Ocha. One of these remains attached to the parent rock and another, 36 ft in length, is the same size as those in the Temple of Antoninus and Faustina in

Ancient cipollino columns at Kylindroi quarry on mount Ocha

Rome. In 1881 the Post Office Directory entry for Brindley's firm, Farmer and Brindley, included the words 'Sole agents for cipollino'. The 1885 entry read 'Sole agents for rediscovered Roman quarries, Numidian, cipollino, pavonazzetto'. Two years later Brindley told the Royal Institute of British Architects that 'Good cipollino is now again obtainable'.

How much cipollino was supplied by Farmer and Brindley is unclear. They were listed as agents for the marble until 1899 when this changed to 'Quarry proprietors of Egyptian Porphyry, antique Greek Cipollino and Rosso Antico'. But two years earlier, in 1897, the Anglo-Greek Marble Company (Marmor), the largest in Europe with capital of £235,000, had been formed to develop quarries at Pentelikon, Paros, Tinos, Skyros, Naxos and Euboea. By 1909 Marmor was advertising as sole suppliers of cipollino 'from the original ancient Greek quarries'. Farmer and Brindley became a private limited company in 1905, when Brindley effectively retired at the age of 74, and any independent involvement in quarrying seems likely to have ended at about that time.

The first recorded consignment of cipollino from Euboea reaching London was in 1898. It was of slabs for the new staircase walls at Drapers' Hall and four columns for the Royal Academy of Arts. Shortly afterwards eight more columns arrived for Westminster Cathedral. The marble merchants were Farmer and Brindley. Two of the columns for the Cathedral cracked while being worked but the remaining six can be seen at the transepts and at the entrance to St Patrick's, St Paul's and St Joseph's Chapels. Imports continued. Norwich Union's 1904 headquarters in Norwich received 16 cipollino columns and eight more went to decorate the 1907 Old Bailey entrance hall. By that time, according to Brindley, over 100 large columns had been produced for Britain, Germany and the USA.

Cipollino produces sound, load-bearing, monolithic columns, as can be seen in the Cathedral. But it also has another quality. Consecutive slabs from a block can be opened out or 'book-matched' to form a continuous and attractive pattern. Cipollino used in this way can be seen in both Santa Sophia in Istanbul and in St Mark's, Venice, but the wealth of cipollino in the Cathedral has produced probably the best examples of this technique in Britain. These can be seen all around the Cathedral, as on the piers of the nave, the 'bridge' above the main confessionals and the walls of St Joseph's Chapel.

In early 1956 it was decided that the nave should be clad with marble, including cipollino, in accordance with the original plans of J F Bentley. Farmer and Brindley were no more and it was Mr Whitehead of John Whitehead and Sons, accompanied by Aelred Bartlett, brother of the Cathedral Sub-Administrator, who went to Euboea to choose the marble. Whiteheads were satisfied with readily available cipollino with straight, parallel lines. But Aelred wanted irregular waves and undulating patterns for opening out, and he insisted on the start of a new quarry face to achieve this. The attractive patterns provided by the cipollino in the nave today are the result.

THE LOST COLUMNS

As you enter the Cathedral an avenue of marble columns stretches out before you – first dark green, four on each side, then eight more in pairs as the nave crosses the transepts, and finally eight great yellow columns supporting the baldacchino over the high altar. You would imagine, if you gave it any thought at all, that these columns were selected by the architect, approved by the Cardinal, ordered, quarried, transported, finished and installed as intended. But it did not happen quite like that – not at all, in fact.

The eight dark green columns you see first are verde antico marble from Thessaly in Greece. The same ancient marble appears throughout Italy, particularly in Rome and Venice, and also in Istanbul in Turkey. After lying disused for well over 1,000 years the quarries were rediscovered near Casambala (Hasambali) by William Brindley in 1889-92 and reopened to provide the columns for the Cathedral. The first five marble blocks had been rough-hewn and transported the 7 miles to the railhead at Larissa, when Turkey occupied Thessaly in April 1897 and held it until June 1898, preventing shipment for over a year. Thus it was that the verde antico columns, on which Cardinal Vaughan had set his heart, were not finally cut, polished and installed until late 1899.

But meantime worse had occurred. When you first look at the eight paired columns where the nave crosses the transepts all seems well. But then you notice that on the left a column of wavy light green Greek cipollino has been paired first with a column of cream and purple Italian breccia and then with one of verde antico – not the lovely dark green verde antico of the nave columns but a lighter, less attractive variety, apparently from a different quarry. Meanwhile on the right, a column of the same verde antico stands beside one of Italian breccia while further on breccia and cipollino are paired. It all looks a bit, well…cobbled together. Can this be the work of J F Bentley, a man renowned for his scrupulous attention to detail?

Yes it was, but something had happened outside his control. To his dismay, at Farmer and Brindley's marble yards at 63 Westminster Bridge Road across the Thames, three columns, two of them cipollino and one of Italian breccia, cracked while they were being worked on. To have ordered, quarried, transported, cut and polished replacements from the same quarries would have taken months. After waiting over a year for his verde antico nave columns the cardinal was in no mood for further long delays. The columns were needed at once for the structure of the building. Besides, if cipollino and Italian breccia were prone to crack could replacements of the same marble be relied on?

What was available, however, were blocks of verde antico, released in 1898 from the log-jam caused by the Turkish occupation. In 1892 William Brindley had discovered no less than ten ancient quarries for this marble near Casambala and in 1896 he had set up the Verde Antico Marble Co, conveniently situated at 34 Victoria Street, to supply it. Verde antico was a marble particularly liked by the cardinal and had proved its durability and load-bearing strength over many centuries. It was most unlikely to crack as the other marbles had.

While cleaning progresses, the line of focus remains undisturbed. The baldacchino, with its eight Veronese marble columns, has been considered 'the best thing about the Cathedral'.

Three of the eight paired transept columns are now of cipollino and three of Italian breccia. A drawing (F65) by Bentley to show the design of the transept column capitals (of which there are four types), shades all four columns a light cipollino-like green. This suggests that four transept columns were intended to be of cipollino and therefore, logically, the remaining four of breccia. It thus confirms that two of the columns which broke were intended for the transepts. So where would they have gone? I believe the present pattern tells us. All three cipollino columns are on the inner (nave) side, blending in with the cipollino-clad piers, while all three Italian breccia columns are on the outer (transept) side, reflecting the more varied marbles of the transept walls. This, I believe, was the planned pattern throughout.

But what of the other cipollino column which cracked and was discarded? There is only one obvious position for it – the aisle leading to the Blessed Sacrament Chapel, a position now occupied by a column of the same light verde antico as in the transepts. A cipollino column here would blend in perfectly with the surrounding cipollino wall cladding. Indeed there is no other obvious position for it, for Bentley's columns are almost always paired – either side by side or (in the case of chapel entrance columns) across the nave – Languedoc with Languedoc, Swiss cipollino with Swiss cipollino, Greek with Greek. An exception is the Holy Souls Chapel where the silver-grey Larvikite entrance column is a fitting prelude for the silver mosaic and grey marble of the interior.

The verde antico column in the Blessed Sacrament aisle was also 'lost' for a time – though it subsequently made a comeback. To facilitate processions moving down the aisle, in 1949 the Cathedral authorities had it removed and replaced by a horizontal steel girder. If you look closely at the wall on either side you can see where. The view of the *Westminster Cathedral Chronicle* that this 'will be welcomed by all', was very far from the case. In 1953 the Cathedral Art Committee, which had lapsed, was reinstituted and the column, which fortunately was still in the builder's yard, was restored. It was said that it had been carefully chosen by Bentley. It was, …up to a point.

Finally to the eight columns of yellow Verona marble carrying the baldacchino. Cardinal Vaughan had a contact, Marius Cantini, who owned onyx quarries near Constantine in Algeria and had supplied Marseilles Cathedral. The cardinal decided on onyx for the baldacchino. In vain did marble merchants tell him that onyx columns greater than 5ft 6in had never been produced. At length, in 1902, soon after Bentley's death, the eight onyx columns arrived. Three were already broken and another badly cracked. Two of the others now support the pediment over Our Lady's altar in Birmingham Oratory. The yellow Verona columns originally planned by Bentley were ordered and arrived without mishap in 1905. His baldacchino, on which he had spent so much effort and which he had described as 'the best thing about the Cathedral' was unveiled on Christmas Eve 1906.

A hundred and fifty years ago, John Ruskin, that great exponent of the Gothic style, compared the columns of a marble-encrusted building to its jewels. There are 130 marble columns in Westminster Cathedral, all of them monoliths, all of them solid, ranging in size from 3–15 ft. They are its jewels.

Blessed Sacrament Chapel aisle photographed in 1949 – minus the verde antico column

VERDE ANTICO

Westminster Cathedral was built in the Byzantine style and among its 100 and more marbles there is one which is truly Byzantine. Verde antico marble was used extensively in Constantinople, capital of the Byzantine Empire, and the ancient quarries which provided it were rediscovered and reopened about 100 years ago to build the Cathedral.

In 1886 William Brindley visited Constantinople and realized that some 75 per cent of the coloured marble in the Byzantine churches and mosques there, notably Santa Sophia (the Church of Holy Wisdom), consisted of dark green verde antico. This suggested a readily available source. All knowledge of the quarries had been lost after the Turks had seized Constantinople in 1453, but many centuries before, when Santa Sophia was opened by Emperor Justinian in 563, his court poet, Paul the Silentiary, had described the building and its marbles. To this description Brindley therefore turned.

Verde antico was described by the poet as 'The marble that the land of Atrax yields, not from some upland glen, but from the level plains; in parts fresh green as the sea or emerald stone, or again like blue cornflowers in grass, with here and there a drift of fallen snow, a sweet mingled contrast on the dark shining surface'. Elsewhere Paul refers to the verde antico columns as Thessalian or from Thessaly – a Greek province 200 miles west of Constantinople across the Aegean Sea. So in the spring of 1887 Brindley set off to search for the quarries there, apparently unaware that their location had been previously noted by a Venetian engineer planning the Thessalian railway.

Returning from an unsuccessful search of the site of ancient Atrax in continuous rain, he suddenly noticed what looked like rounded boulders of verde antico set into houses in the town of Larissa. An elderly local Turk told him they were gathered in the fields of the plain, which lies below the foothills of Mount Ossa. Before returning to England Brindley paid a French road engineer to organize a search for signs of old quarries in these hills. But it was not until 1889, after Brindley had sent out sketches he had made of the areas he regarded as most promising, that the first quarry was found, embedded in shale and overlaid with limestone, some 300ft above the plain.

After receiving full particulars by post, Brindley began negotiations through his agent to reopen the quarry. When these were finally completed he returned to Greece in 1892, only to find not less than ten ancient quarries producing every shade and variety of the verde antico marble to be seen in Constantinople and Rome. They also showed the ancient methods of working, one large quarry face consisting of vertical, almost semicircular, hollows where columns, quite probably for Santa Sophia itself, had been axed around prior to being severed at the base. Elsewhere quarry faces and blocks revealed the marks of saws while one quarry contained a block prepared as a 9ft-long sarcophagus.

The quarries are near Casambala (Hasambali), 7 miles north-east of Larissa on the right of the road to Sikourio. Setting up a company and workforce to clear almost 60ft of rubble and reopen them took four years. In 1896 the Verde Antico Marble Company was established with £20,000 capital at 34 Victoria Street and quarrying began. The first five columns to be extracted since the age of Justinian, hand-quarried as in his time, were transported across the plain to the railhead at Larissa towards their final destination in Westminster Cathedral. But then another delay occurred when, in April 1897, Greece attacked Turkey which retaliated by invading Thessaly, taking Larissa and very nearly the Greek crown prince.

Although the war lasted only a week, negotiations over war reparations to Turkey lasted a year. It was not until June 1898 that the Turks finally withdrew, allowing the verde antico columns to leave the railway sidings at Larissa and travel down to the port at Volos, and from there to Farmer and Brindley's marble works at 63 Westminster Bridge Road, London. There they were turned on a large lathe with steel blades, ground with sand and polished with oxide of tin, finally being put in place in the Cathedral in late 1899 – 13 years after William Brindley had started his quest in 1886.

With verde antico again available, demand increased. Blocks measuring thousands of cubic feet were cut direct from the quarry face using a wire saw, and columns were installed in the hall of the Old Bailey and the Norwich Union head-quarters, Norwich. The Cathedral received eleven verde antico columns, which stand between the nave and the aisles and transepts, though at 13ft they are dwarfed by the 48 great columns of Santa Sophia between 22ft and 25ft 6in in height. Elsewhere in the Cathedral verde antico panels can be seen in the nave and organ screen, in the sanctuary and apse and in all but one of the chapels. The marble was last used to decorate the entrance porches in 1963-4 and for Cardinal Heenan's tomb in 1976. The Verde Antico Marble Company was wound up in 1912 but others took over, quarrying by a Greek company (Tsalmas Marmi) continuing until 1985.

Classified as an ophicalcite breccia, from the Greek word 'ophis' meaning snake, verde antico is composed of angular pieces of green and black serpentine and white calcite, all cemented together in a lighter green matrix. It is both beautiful and able to bear great weights safely. It was quarried in Thessaly from at least the age of Hadrian in the early second century AD to that of Justinian in the sixth. Besides Santa Sophia and other Istanbul churches, such as that of Sergius and Bacchus, there are 24 columns in the nave of St John Lateran in Rome while others contrast with purple porphyry in the facade of St Mark's, Venice. In all there are perhaps 600 columns of the marble in Europe, over 200 in Rome and eleven in the Cathedral – the first to be quarried for more than 1,300 years.

ROSSO ANTICO

One of the most prominent of the Cathedral's marbles is rosso antico. It can be seen immediately on entering the Cathedral, forming the deep red screen and steps which divide the sanctuary from the nave. Rosso antico is also used to decorate the marble floor near the main entrance and that in the Holy Souls Chapel, the east wall (above and beside the altar) of St George's Chapel and the walls and floor of the Lady Chapel. The colour ranges from purple to violet, sometimes banded with white stripes and black veins. It appears lighter when unpolished, as when used on the floor or steps. It comes from the Mani, the remote and mountainous central spur of the Greek mainland which reaches out southwards into the Mediterranean Sea.

There are two areas where the marble has been quarried. The first, where outcrops of the white-banded variety meet the sea at Paganea, near Skutari, in the outer Mani, was rediscovered by a French scientific expedition in the 1830s. They named it 'Marbre rouge antique de Skutari'. Specimens of this marble were sent by Greece to the Great Exhibition in London in 1851, but its use elsewhere seems to have been limited. More recently, quarrying took place at Paganea from about 1950 until 1964 and the plain, dark red marble used to decorate the transept piers in the Cathedral during this period appears to be from there.

The main quarries lie in the deep Mani. Boulders of rosso antico can be seen on Cape Tenaro (also known as Cape Matapan), where the Taygetos Mountains finally run into the sea. But it is 7 miles inland, close to the deserted village of Profitis Ilias, where several quarries, some ancient, can be found and where the hilltops and the village itself stand above huge mounds of purple marble rubble. The pedestal for a statue of Lord Byron, presented by the Greek government and erected at Hyde Park Corner in 1881, was said to be from the quarries at Cape Matapan and rosso antico panels were also used on the floor of the Oxford Examination Schools building, completed in 1882.

In 1887 Farmer and Brindley were advertising rosso antico 'from rediscovered quarries of Greece'. They were listed as quarry proprietors of the marble from 1899-1907 when the firm of Marmor Ltd seems to have taken over. Farmer and Brindley completed the Cathedral sanctuary screen in 1906 and the Lady Chapel in 1908 and the marble used appears identical to that at Cape Tenaro and Profitis Ilias.

But of course rosso antico was used long before the nineteenth century. Indeed the term 'antico' indicates its use in Classical times. Carved blocks decorated the Treasury of Atreus in thirteenth-century BC Mycenae. But it was during the Roman Empire, particularly under Hadrian in the second century AD, that rosso antico was most popular, both for buildings and for sculpture – notably a bust of a priest and several statues of fauns (companions of Bacchus, the god of wine). Much Roman rosso antico was later reused, as in the sanctuary steps of the church of Santa Prassede in Rome.

The stone continues to be used in the Mani. It can be seen set into churches, private houses and even garden walls. But overgrown tracks and long abandoned quarries show that overseas demand has moved on. It seems not inappropriate that here in the Cathedral this ancient purple marble, associated with ritual and red wine, should decorate the entrance to the sanctuary, where Mass is celebrated.

The main rosso antico quarry face at Profitis Ilias, Cape Tenaro

PURPLE PORPHYRY

Purple porphyry is the most valuable of all the Cathedral's marbles. Known to the Romans as lapis porphyrites and to the Byzantines as the Stone of Rome, the quarries were imperial property and the porphyry itself reserved for the Roman emperors. But many of the men who worked in the quarries were Christian prisoners, and over the years porphyry came to signify the Sacrifice of Christ and Christian martyrdom.

The name porphyry is derived from the Latin *purpureus*, meaning purple, the imperial colour. It is dark purplish red spotted with white crystals and is an igneous rock, molten magma formed at very high temperatures in the earth's interior, which has cooled and solidified below the surface. The quarries are situated some 4,000ft up Gebel Dokhan, in Egypt's Eastern Desert. An unpaved Roman road linked them to Keneh, 96 miles to the south-west on a bend of the Nile near Thebes, and to the Red Sea port of Myos Hormos, 25 miles to the north-east.

To these quarries at Gebel Dokhan, Mons Porphyrites to the Romans, were sent Christian and other convicted prisoners. At the quarry face porphyry blocks were split away along a line of deep incisions (cut by chisel), by inserting metal or wooden wedges, the latter then being soaked with water to make them swell. The blocks were then shaped with chisels and lowered down the steep mountain ravines, probably on wooden sledges tethered by ropes to solid stone piers placed a few paces apart on either side. Once on level ground the porphyry blocks were loaded on wagons to be pulled by oxen the 100 miles or so down to the Nile and from there by water to Alexandria and thence to Rome.

The settlement has not been fully excavated but coins, inscriptions and written records indicate that the quarries were worked at least as early as the reign of the Emperor Claudius in the first century AD. Work continued even after Constantine's legalization of Christianity in 313 had greatly reduced the supply of Christian convicts. But this, coupled with increasing external pressure on the boundaries of the Roman Empire, finally led to the settlement being abandoned at some stage between 350 and 450 AD, all the signs being that the exodus was hurried.

For 1,400 years Mons Porphyrites was known only to the Bedouin. It was rediscovered by the British explorers Burton and Wilkinson in 1822-3. Sir Gardner Wilkinson made detailed notes and plans and sent back samples of porphyry to England. Others followed and in 1887 William Brindley also set off for the quarries. Leaving Keneh with his wife, 19 attendants and 15 camels, he reached the mountain in six days and, following old Roman tracks, climbed up to the quarries where he found porphyry of every description and variety, some partly wedged from the face. On returning to Keneh and then to Cairo, Brindley negotiated a concession to rework the quarries.

Brindley planned to use Myos Hormos, only 25 miles away, to send the porphyry through the Suez Canal to England. But the combination of the great hardness of the rock and its location, the absence of sufficient water and the availability of only rock-strewn and partly washed away Roman roads, proved insurmountable. By 1907 the quarries had still not been worked and Brindley was calling on others to take on the challenge. But it was only in 1989 that an English sculptor, Stephen Cox, returned to Gebel Dokhan to obtain porphyry for the new Cairo Opera House. Cox has continued to work in Egypt and has produced several more works in porphyry including the altar, font, consecration crosses and Stations of the Cross for St Paul's Church, Haringey, in 1993.

In the first century AD the elder Pliny wrote that the porphyry quarries of Egypt could furnish blocks of any dimension, however large. The Emperor Constantine's column in Constantinople (still standing though much damaged) was 100ft high, made up of nine cylindrical drums each 11ft in height and diameter. Two centuries later, eight columns almost 40ft high were used to decorate the Church of Santa Sophia, Constantinople, sent to the Emperor Justinian from Valerian's Temple of the Sun in Rome. Smaller columns decorate the façade of St Mark's, Venice, with more porphyry used for the pulpits. There are some 300 porphyry columns in Europe (mainly in Rome), numerous sarcophagi and innumerable slabs, including a circular one 8ft 6in across on the floor of St Peter's, Rome.

In the twelfth and thirteenth centuries, the Cosmati family of stonemasons revived the ancient art of *opus sectile* in Rome by cutting up old marble to form patterns on church floors and furniture. The designs centred on roundels, usually of porphyry, and the practice was widely copied. In Westminster Cathedral the pulpit (originally made in Rome) and the floor of St Paul's Chapel are decorated with porphyry roundels, panels and chips in the Cosmatesque manner. The altar in St Paul's and the floor of St Joseph's are also inset with porphyry while panels decorate the east and west walls of St Patrick's and the east wall of St Andrew's. According to the *Westminster Cathedral Chronicle* of September 1928, when the west wall of St Patrick's had just been decorated, the two panels of purple porphyry there were cut from a block brought to England by Lord Elgin and credibly reputed to have come from the Temple of Diana (Artemis) at Ephesus. If so, they could well have witnessed the riot caused by the activities of St Paul in that city (Acts 19). A single slim porphyry column is used as a lectern in the sanctuary of the Cathedral.

CARRARA

When marble is mentioned many people will think of the structures of ancient Rome. Others may remember the buildings and sculptures of the Renaissance, London's Marble Arch or churchyard monuments. Most of these originated in the Carrara region of Italy, the world's largest producer of white marble. But the area produces 60 varieties of marble, some coloured, and many of them can be found in Westminster Cathedral.

Carrara lies between the mountains and the sea in north-west Tuscany. The main quarries are in the Colonnata, Fantiscritti and Ravaccione valleys but the marble mountains of the Apuan Alps stretch 20 miles from Carrara in the west to the villages of Seravezza and Stazzema to the east. The marble was formed some 200 million years ago from the remains of marine creatures accumulating on the seabed. Gradually these became exceptionally pure limestone. About 50 million years ago the European and African continental shelves forced the region downwards and immense heat and pressure recrystallized (metamorphosed) the limestone into shining white marble which later rose to form the Apuan Alps.

Fine-grained statuary marble is found in stratified beds all along this mountain range. In Westminster Cathedral it was used for the column capitals, each one of which took two stonemasons from Farmer and Brindley three months to carve, using chisels and hand-drills in situ. White statuary marble from Carrara was also used for the base and superstructure of the baldacchino, which stands on eight columns of yellow Verona marble above the high altar, and the relief carving of St Michael in the Shrine of the Sacred Heart and St Michael. More recently a variety of Carrara marble called acqua bianca (white water) was used for Cardinal Hume's tomb in the Chapel of St Gregory and St Augustine.

Most marble from the Carrara region is not, in fact, pure white. Veining and shading results from the presence of mineral impurities during formation. Lightly veined second statuary was used for the marble floor of the Cathedral while the more heavily veined arabescato is on the walls and floor of St George's Chapel. Below the stratified beds of white and white vein marble in the mountains, lie beds of a generally blue-grey colour. The darker grey were known in England as 'doves' and examples can be seen at the corners of the Chapel of the Holy Souls. Lighter blue-grey marble, traversed by darker veins, is bardiglio fiorito. It paves the narthex floor and is on the walls and floor in the Holy Souls.

Great earth movements millions of years ago also resulted in fragmentation of the marble, allowing water-borne minerals to penetrate and stain it a variety of colours before it gradually resolidified. Thus the breccias were formed. Columns of breccia di Seravezza front the organ loft above the narthex and are paired with green verde antico and cipollino columns at the transepts. Breccia violetta, of a more pronounced violet hue and also from Seravezza, can be seen on the walls of the entrance lobbies and set into the baldacchino. Finally, as if to demonstrate the variety of marbles from the Seravezza area, a column of fior di pesco (peach blossom) marble stands against the wall in St Joseph's Chapel, while one of blue bardilla stands opposite in St Paul's.

CARRARA

The ancient Etruscan-Roman port of Luni, or Luna, about 5 miles west of modern Carrara, was founded in 177 BC and was the centre of the local marble industry in Roman times. Luna marble was in large-scale use in Rome by 36 BC and about ten years earlier, Mamurra, who lived on the Coelian Hill, was the first to have only solid marble columns in his whole house, these being of Carystus or Luna marble. Mamurra was Julius Caesar's prefect of works and probably organized the exploitation of the quarries for his building programme. Subsequently Emperor Augustus used the marble extensively for temples and other buildings in Rome. For the next 150 years Luna supplied most of Rome's white marble, examples of its use being Trajan's Column and that of Marcus Aurelius, both well over 100ft high. From the late second century AD onwards, however, more costly marbles from overseas, notably Proconnesian and Pentelic, came to predominate.

For 1,000 years the Carrara quarries were largely deserted until again being extensively used in the Renaissance. Duke Cosimo de' Medici in Florence was anxious to exploit the mineral wealth of Tuscany and Michelangelo made many extended visits to the Carrara mountains in search of the finest statuary marble. To his dismay, in 1518 Pope Leo X sent him to the unexploited Monte Altissimo region above Seravezza for marble for the façade of the Medici church of San Lorenzo in Florence. In the event San Lorenzo remained unclad brickwork but marble from the region was used for both the Duomo in Florence and St Peter's Basilica in Rome, as well as for Michelangelo's most famous sculptures such as his Pietà, Moses and David.

There are 200-300 active marble quarries in the Carrara region, less than half the number of a century ago. But mechanization has resulted in around a million tons of marble being produced annually, mostly for the Middle East. Until the end of the nineteenth century it was quarried with pickaxes, chisels and wedges and allowed to slide down the mountains on wooden sledges before being carried away by bullock wagon – practices unchanged since Roman times. Only in 1895 was the endless wire saw, constantly fed with sand and water, introduced into the quarries. Meanwhile in the town of Carrara, the main processing centre, marble blocks are now sawn into slabs for walls and floors using diamond-bladed saws, and full-size marble statues are created from the plaster models of sculptors.

A stonemason carving a column capital from a block of white statuary marble

CORK RED

There are at least four Irish marbles in Westminster Cathedral. Of these by far the most prominent is the mottled red marble which can be seen on the back wall above the wooden cabinets, beside the information desk, on the inner face of the nave piers and in many of the chapels – notably St Patrick's. Although the Cathedral was far from the first to use it, it was almost certainly the last.

Cork red is an unusual and attractive limestone made up of pebbles, some grey but most stained varying shades of red by iron oxide, set in a deeper red matrix. A range of fossils can be seen, mainly crinoids (sea-lilies), but also other marine creatures such as molluscs. It was formed in the Lower Carboniferous period (330-360 million years ago) when a grey limestone reef beneath the warm, shallow sea then covering the region was buried beneath red sediment, carried by currents or perhaps resulting from a tilting of the sea floor.

Cork red marble, known in the past also as Victoria red, was quarried near Fermoy and Buttevant, at Midleton and nearby Baneshane, and at Boreenmanagh, Churchtown and Little Island close to Cork city. The marble was known by 1850, when examples (still on show) were displayed in the foyer of the Museum of Economic Geology in Dublin. From then on it was used to decorate many important buildings such as the Museum of Trinity College in Dublin, the Oxford University Natural History Museum, the Liverpool and Manchester Exchanges, St Finbarre's Cathedral in Cork, and St Colman's in Cobh, both of which possess great columns of the marble. But World War I and the Troubles disrupted both building and trade and the Cork red quarries, by then largely exhausted, fell into disuse.

Westminster Cathedral has the marble in the nave and the inner crypt and also on the floor of the sanctuary, the Lady Chapel (either side of the altar) and near the niches outside the Blessed Sacrament Chapel. The altar table in the Sacred Heart Shrine is also of Cork red while in St Patrick's Chapel it can be seen in the altar frontal, the floor and the little columns lining the wall below the windows. All the marble appears to be from the same source. Geological Survey of Ireland records show that Cork red from Baneshane Quarry was used in the Cathedral about 1910. Farmer and Brindley were responsible for the marblework in the Cathedral at that time and are likely to have used only one quarry for the Cork red they needed. They returned in the 1920s to lay the floor and erect the columns in St Patrick's, probably using pre-war stock.

Baneshane Quarry, 150ft long, 60ft wide and 15ft deep, lies in the County Cork countryside, 12 miles to the east of Cork city and 1 mile west of the market town of Midleton. Open by 1850, in 1914 it seems to have been abandoned and allowed to fill with water which was used to irrigate local fields. But in early 1956, after much discussion in the Cathedral Art Committee, it was resolved that the nave of the Cathedral should be clad with marble in line with the original designs. By now Farmer and Brindley were no more and the marble merchants chosen, John Whitehead and Sons, recommended a salmon-pink Portuguese marble for the red needed.

It was Aelred Bartlett, artist and brother of Francis, the future Administrator of the Cathedral, who rejected this proposal and who approached the Irish Embassy in London to see if Cork red marble was still obtainable. With the help of the Geological Survey of Ireland, Aelred travelled to Baneshane Quarry on 12 April 1956. The quarry was inspected, drained and reopened and, from 1956-64 the Cathedral nave and narthex received its marble cladding, including the Cork red last put in place 30 years before – the red of Baneshane. Since then, despite the potential for further development, the quarry has again been abandoned, overgrown with briars, gorse and maturing trees. Now forgotten by almost all, at least it will be remembered in Westminster Cathedral.

CONNEMARA GREEN

The green marble of Connemara is an ophicalcite, extremely varied both in colour and pattern. It is known as Connemara green or Irish green. It is also very old. It comes from quarries in the neighbourhood of Clifden, the capital of Connemara, and its history is interwoven with the history and development of that town.

Connemara green marble was originally a lime mud formed in shallow seas in the Precambrian period, some 600 million years ago. About 100 million years later it was metamorphosed, recrystallized under immense heat and pressure, and new minerals such as serpentine, chlorite and mica developed. It is these minerals that give the marble its characteristic and attractive variety of patterns and colours – a unique combination of bands, veins and patches of green, yellow, brown, white and grey.

In 1804, John D'Arcy, aged only 19, inherited large estates in Connemara, then largely cut off from the outside world. He described his tenants as 'A rare breed of people, wild like the mountains they inhabit'. By 1812 he had resolved to establish a town and seaport there, with roads linking it to Galway and Westport. From his new home in Clifden Castle, west of Clifden, he badgered the government in Dublin Castle for money to relieve local poverty and unemployment by building piers and roads, while offering permanent leases of land to those prepared to settle in the area. By 1826 a prosperous modern town had been created at Clifden, trading directly with Liverpool and elsewhere.

Meanwhile, 2 miles north of Clifden, close to the turn off for the Sky Road and Streamstown Bay, John D'Arcy was developing a small quarry of banded dark and light green marble. From Streamstown the marble blocks were carted by a new road to Clifden for shipment from the newly-built pier. On his death in 1839, John's son, Hyacinth, continued to work the quarry, but the Great Famine of 1845-9 ruined the family and resulted in the sale of their estates, including the quarry, to Thomas Eyre of Bath. Hyacinth D'Arcy joined the Church of Ireland and became Rector of Clifden, building a new church there in 1853.

By this time Connemara marble was becoming well known. In the early 1840s two English travellers, the Halls, wrote glowingly of it and purchased a slab measuring 3ft x 2ft for £3/l0s. A book by Sir Robert Kane in 1844 referred to marble from the D'Arcy quarries at Streamstown being exported in considerable quantities. A few years later, in 1850, panels of Connemara were displayed in Dublin's Museum of Economic Geology, with columns in the Museum of Trinity College nearby, while in England columns of the marble were used for Oxford's University Museum of Natural History.

Clifden pier was used extensively until 1895, when a railway linked the town with Galway. In the same year Streamstown Quarry was acquired by Robert Fisher of New York and large amounts of marble exported for American churches and public buildings. It was also much used in England – perhaps most extravagantly in the new General Post Office at King Edward's Buildings in the City of London, opened in 1910. More recently, in 1981, Pope John Paul II was presented with an 18in Celtic cross and candlesticks of Streamstown marble on behalf of the youth of Ireland. The light green, dark green and sepia varieties of Streamstown marble continue to be marketed by Connemara Marble Industries from its factory and showroom at Moycullen, near Galway city.

In the Cathedral, slabs of this green marble, with its attractive figuring, can be seen on the east wall, altar and floor of St Patrick's Chapel, and also on the floor of St Andrew's and the Baptistry. Celtic designs on the floor of St Patrick's, and leaves and wreaths on that in the Lady Chapel, show dark Streamstown alternating and contrasting with the yellower marble from Barnanoraun Quarry. This lies in the Owenglin valley, 6 miles east of Clifden, and the marble there has wilder and more tangled patterns than that of Streamstown. The yellowish-green panels on the floor of the Vaughan Chantry may also be from Barnanoraun.

Barnanoraun Quarry formed part of the estate of the Martins of Ballynahinch Castle and the marble, also called Ballynahinch marble, was carted the 5 miles over a steep ridge down to Ballynahinch and Cloonisle pier for shipment. The quarry has been in operation from at least the early nineteenth century, its marble being described by Sir C L Giesecke to the Royal Dublin Society in 1826. It also appears in the museum buildings of Trinity College and Oxford University. Today Joyces Marble Quarries markets blocks, gallets, slabs and tiles of Barnanoraun marble from a factory at Recess, 9 miles down the road from Clifden, and a nearby craft shop sells carved marble articles to visitors.

Probably the most beautiful example of Connemara marble in the Cathedral appears in the centre of the altar frontal in St Joseph's Chapel. This translucent, clouded green panel comes from Lissoughter Quarry on the south-west slope of Lissoughter Hill, just above Recess. Other examples are the light green diamonds high on the walls of the Lady Chapel. Elsewhere in London, Lissoughter green can be seen in the hotel and booking office of St Pancras Station. Originally worked to a small extent by the Martins of Ballynahinch, in 1870 the Dublin firm of Sibthorpe took over and began extensive production. But despite the beauty of the marble, it is troublesome to work and the quarry is now used only occasionally to produce random blocks for tiles and giftware.

IONA GREEN

One of the most unusual of the Cathedral's marbles is Scottish, from a tiny quarry, long disused, on the island of Iona, in the Hebrides. Iona green marble can be seen on the floor of the Chapel of St Andrew, patron saint of Scotland. It is predominantly white, flecked with light and dark green, and is inlaid here with 29 fish and other marine creatures. The marble was put in place in 1913-15 by Farmer and Brindley at the expense of the Fourth Marquess of Bute.

Geologically, Iona green is a true marble in which the original limestone has been recrystallized under great heat and pressure. The quarry lies almost at the southernmost point of Iona, in a valley beside the sea just to the east of St Columba's Bay. Translucent green pebbles of the marble are thrown up by the sea in nearby bays and are known as 'mermaids' tears', from the legend that a match between a mermaid and an Iona monk was prevented by King Neptune and the abbot.

It seems probable that intermittent quarrying of Iona green has occurred from at least medieval times. By the end of the seventeenth century writers were referring to a marble altar table in Iona Abbey, on the other side of the island. This was destroyed in the eighteenth century as a result of a local belief that possession of a fragment would protect against shipwrecks, fire and miscarriages, but today both the modern altar table and font base are of Iona green marble. In the late eighteenth century quarrying again took place, organized by the Duke of Argyll, and quantities of marble were sent to Leith and London before extraction and transport problems put an end to the venture.

The marble for St Andrew's Chapel was quarried by the Iona Marble Company, formed in 1906. This operated with up to 12 men until World War I put a stop to operations. The Secretary of the Company went off to fight and many of the quarrymen will have done the same. So there the quarry lies today, scattered blocks and fragments of marble, cutting machinery for slabs, and footings for the derricks which used to swing the marble onto Glasgow-bound vessels, all now frozen in time.

The quarry on Iona, as it lies today, idle rusting machinery with scattered blocks and fragments of marble

DERBYSHIRE FOSSIL AND HOPTON WOOD

Perhaps surprisingly, of all the marbles in Westminster Cathedral, only two come from England and Wales. These are Derbyshire fossil and Hopton Wood, limestones originally laid down in shallow tropical seas in what today is the Peak District of Derbyshire.

The two marbles are composed of fragments of marine life such as shells, corals and animal debris, which gradually accumulated on the sea floor to a depth of thousands of feet. At that time, in the Carboniferous period some 330 million years ago, Britain was 5°–10° south of the Equator, rather than 50° degrees north as today, and the region would have looked like a series of Pacific Ocean reefs surrounding a lagoon.

The most attractive example of Derbyshire fossil marble in the Cathedral is the skirting between St Paul's and St Andrew's Chapels. Light grey-brown in colour, it contains an abundance of fossilized sea creatures, notably crinoids. These sea-lilies consist of a flower-like structure supported by a jointed stem attached to the sea floor. A series of hard rings surround and protect the stem and these, called 'St Cuthbert's Beads' and used to make rosaries, can be seen clearly. The rings also resemble the eye of a bird – hence 'bird's-eye marble'. The example here is from Coal Hills quarry near Wirksworth, in production by the mid-nineteenth century but now abandoned and part of the National Stone Centre.

The other examples of Derbyshire fossil in the Cathedral are darker. A brown variety with less obvious fossils is used for the column bases and retaining walls either side of the sanctuary. Then some 50 years ago, from 1956-64, the nave piers and narthex received their marble cladding and, once again, dark Derbyshire fossil was chosen for the skirting. This is an almost black variety and appears to come from Dene Quarry on the outskirts of Cromford, close to Wirksworth. The quarry was first used in 1942 but by 1960 production difficulties and reduced demand had resulted in a concentration on producing crushed stone for road-building, which continues today.

Like Derbyshire fossil, Hopton Wood marble is used extensively in the Cathedral. It ranges from a rich cream to a dark grey or fawn, depending on its position in the quarry and the number of fossils, largely crinoids. Of uniform texture it is a compact stone of great hardness which can be used internally and externally. It was first extracted at Hopton Wood in the mid-eighteenth century and employed extensively for flooring and staircases in the rebuilding of Kedleston Hall near Derby in the 1760s and 1770s. To cope with increasing demand for what became a fashionable stone, quarries were opened at nearby Middleton, close to Wirksworth, where production was centred.

In the Cathedral, Hopton Wood marble is seen in the arches either side of the sanctuary and around the reliquaries and windows in the crypt. In St Paul's Chapel the two piscinas, put in place either side of the altar in 1914-15, are also of this marble, decorated with red and white inlay and given a high polish. In the aisles near the Cathedral entrance the holy water stoups, each surmounted by a carved shell and dating from 1918, demonstrate that Hopton Wood is virtually impervious to water. Here they have been given a light 'eggshell' polish. And, as if to demonstrate its versatility, the same marble, inlaid with red and green porphyry this time, was laid on the floor of St Joseph's Chapel in 1939.

But the best-known Hopton Wood marble in the Cathedral is undoubtedly that used for the Stations of the Cross. Eric Gill used stone of various types for his sculptures, among them Bath, Beer and Portland. But Hopton Wood seems to have been his favourite. He is recorded as taking his apprentices up to Wirksworth to select blocks, and both at the start and at the end of his career he used Hopton Wood – for the Cathedral Stations in 1914-18 and for the altarpiece in St George's Chapel in 1939-40. Appropriately enough, his memorial below the Fourteenth Station is also of Hopton Wood.

So why were British marbles not used more extensively in the Cathedral? Why do we not have the green of Anglesey, the red and white of Plymouth and Totnes, the swirling red-black and green of Cornish Lizard serpentine? Firstly, because the Cathedral is in the Byzantine style and many of the marbles here are those used in Byzantine churches. Secondly, the main marble decorator for the Cathedral, William Brindley, had personally located and reopened ancient quarries in Greece, Turkey and Egypt and wanted to exploit them. And finally, because of differing production and transport costs, it was quite simply cheaper to import Continental marble by sea than to raise and convey marble from British quarries by train.

A TOUR OF THE MARBLES

Over 100 different varieties of marble decorate Westminster Cathedral (125 at the last count), almost certainly more than in any other building in England. They come from 23 countries on five continents and many of them were used in ancient Greece and Rome.

On entering the Cathedral by the main entrance you are likely to be standing on light blue-grey bardiglio fiorito (flowered blue) from the Carrara area of Tuscany. Immediately in front are two red columns, a reminder that the Cathedral is dedicated to the Precious Blood. They are of Swedish Imperial red granite with bases of dark grey Norwegian Larvikite showing iridescent flecks of silvery mica, and with capitals of carved Carrara statuary marble. All the nave column capitals were meticulously designed by J F Bentley in the Byzantine style.

Looking down the nave the dark green columns on either side are verde antico from Thessaly in Greece. They come from a series of ancient quarries which supplied the columns for Byzantine churches such as Santa Sophia and Sergius and Bacchus in Constantinople. Between the columns are great brick-built piers. The smaller are clad with Greek cipollino from the Island of Euboea, used extensively in ancient Rome. The larger are faced with Cork red from near Midleton in Co Cork, Ireland, and Campan vert from the Commune of Campan, near Lourdes in the French Pyrenees.

Moving to the right down the south aisle you come to the Chapel of St Gregory and St Augustine. Most of the marbles here are Italian – a lovely panel of white Carrara on the floor above Cardinal Hume's tomb, yellow and black Tuscan breccia below the windows and veined dark red rosso di Levanto from Liguria for the bench below. The altar frontal is also from Italy, exceptionally beautiful slabs of yellow Siena, but the great twin entrance columns are waxy Swiss cipollino from the Canton Valais, while the altar table is Norwegian pink from Fauske, with the rather attractive title of 'Midnight Sun' – you can see why.

On now to the Chapel of St Patrick where Irish marbles are much employed – wavy green Connemara for the altar frontal and floor, Cork red for the little columns below the windows, the centre of the altar frontal and also much of the floor, and Kilkenny black fossil marble for the altar top. But marbles from many other countries also appear. Below the altar is a design combining turquoise amazonite from Colorado with dark blue Chilean lapis lazuli in a surround of green verdite from Pemberton in the Transvaal. Above the niches either side of the altar, French red Languedoc encloses diamonds of red and grey africano marble – certainly ancient since the old Roman quarry, near Izmir in Turkey, had flooded, become a lake and remained undiscovered until 1966.

Passing between more panels of yellow and black Tuscan breccia we come to St Andrew's Chapel with its 'pavement like the sea'. Besides being the patron saint of Scotland, St Andrew was a fisherman so the floor uses marble to remind us of this. The central floor panels are swirling purple and white Arni fantastico from Tuscany. The surrounding dark green wave is Connemara and the light green and white marble, which contains 29 sea creatures, is from the Iona marble quarry in Scotland. This closed in World War I but the workings and machinery can still be seen. The altar in St Andrew's

Installing panels of yellow Siena marble on a nave pier in 1959

consists of three Scottish granites – the table of Alloa, the pillars of red Peterhead and the base of Aberdeen.

An English marble can be seen between St Andrew's and St Paul's Chapels. The skirting here is light grey Derbyshire fossil from Wirksworth and contains a myriad of sea creatures. The grey piscinas either side of the altar in St Paul's are also from Wirksworth – Hopton Wood stone this time. But the main marbles in this chapel are Turkish and Greek. Grey and white banded Proconnesian from the Turkish Island of Marmara lines the wall behind the altar, which is of translucent white Pentelic from Mount Pentelikon near Athens – used to build the Parthenon. Dusky grey Hymettian, also from near Athens, lines the walls.

The floor of St Paul's Chapel provides another attraction. It combines Greek green porphyry and verde antico with Egyptian purple porphyry in a nice example of Cosmatesque work. The nearby pulpit, and the delightful floor panel (designed by Aelred Bartlett) below the statue of Our Lady of Westminster, are also in the Cosmatesque style. In the twelfth and thirteenth centuries the Cosmati, a Roman family and guild of marble and mosaic workers, cut up and assembled pieces of coloured marble from the ruins of Imperial Rome to produce decorative patterns on floors, pulpits, and episcopal thrones. The style was widely copied, being known as Cosmatesque.

Before the Lady Chapel stand two imposing red columns from Languedoc in France. The lower walls in the chapel display pink-flushed giallo antico from Kleber in Algeria and dark red rosso antico from the Mani in southern Greece. Next door, in the sanctuary, the side columns behind the wooden stalls are also French, rouge jaspe from near Toulon, alternating with Norwegian pink. But the column capitals remain uncarved. The high altar, 12 tons of Cornish granite, stands beneath its canopy, or baldacchino, of white Carrara inlaid with coloured marbles, resting on eight columns of yellow Verona. Looking back down the nave, the latest (1995) marbles can be seen fronting the piers at gallery level – dark red rosso Laguna from Turkey and light blue azul Macaubas from Brazil.

Another marble from Kleber, the deeper pink, rose de Numidie, lines the walls in the Blessed Sacrament Chapel, together with yellow Siena. Further on, the Vaughan Chantry encloses the effigy and empty tomb of Cardinal Vaughan in carved white Pentelic. Two striking black and white columns, known as grand antique des Pyrénées or bianco e nero, stand outside. This French marble from Aubert, Ariège was also used in Roman and Byzantine buildings. Next, to St Joseph's Chapel, where slabs of cipollino, cut from the same block, have been opened out to create attractive patterns. In front of them are little colonnettes of onyx with a central column of Tuscan fior di pesco, peach-blossom marble.

Next door is the Chapel of St George and the English Martyrs, so many of the marbles are red – Greek rosso antico inlaid with mother-of-pearl roses on the wall above the altar, rouge sanguine from Kleber on the altar frontal, with dark red French rouge griotte (called partridge-eye because of its pearly white spots or eyes) on the floor, with a red English rose of rosso antico in the centre. The final chapel is that of the Holy Souls, with its themes of death and mourning. Here the colours are subdued – an entrance column of silver-grey Norwegian Larvikite with floor and walls of grey bardiglio fiorito and dark green verde di mare (green of the sea) from Genoa. And so we come to the bronze statue of St Peter, the rock on which our Church is founded, and are back to where we started.

Marble revetment of the nave arcading and gallery balustrade in 1959

The nave in 1964. The marble revetment is finally complete and it will be another
30 years before more panels are installed – for the 1995 centenary.

CATHEDRAL MOSAICS
MOSAICS AND METHODS

Only a small part of the Cathedral has yet received its mosaics – above the main entrance and a side entrance, seven of the 12 chapels, the great sanctuary arch and the smaller arch in the crypt, together with a few panels elsewhere. Yet already over 12 million pieces of mosaic have been laid. To complete the decoration in the manner originally intended – as illustrated in the 1950 artist's impression at the back of the Cathedral – would require up to 100 million.

Mosaic consists of small pieces of marble, stone, terracotta or glass (known as tesserae or smalti) applied to a prepared surface. When the practice first began is unclear but in the fourth millennium BC coloured clay cones were being pressed into damp mud to decorate buildings in Mesopotamia and by the start of the fourth century BC coloured pebbles were being used by the Greeks to produce regular patterns and representations of human figures and animals. The Romans used mosaic extensively for floors and in the first century BC they began decorating the walls of their imitation grottoes with marble chips, sea-shells and ultimately stone and glass tesserae. In the first century AD the use of decorative coloured glass on walls increased but it was the Christians who applied the technique most extensively and successfully – notably in the fifth and sixth centuries in the churches of Constantinople and Ravenna, in the twelfth and thirteenth in those of Palermo, Monreale and Cefalù in Sicily, together with St Mark's in Venice, and in Rome from the fourth to the thirteenth centuries.

The opaque glass tesserae used in the Cathedral average 1sq cm and come mainly from Venice and the island of Murano nearby. Some have gold or silver leaf fused on to clear glass with another thin sheet of glass on top to protect the metal from the atmosphere. On average 700 tesserae are used to the square foot, so the blue sanctuary arch mosaic consists of over a million and the Lady Chapel has about 3 million. The first mosaics were designed for the Holy Souls Chapel by the artist W C Symons and it was only here that J F Bentley played a direct part, urging that a simple Greek style should be adopted and designing two garlands himself.

The mosaics of the Holy Souls above the altar portray the journey of the souls through purgatory, where the archangels Raphael and Michael stand, to Paradise at the top. On the opposite wall are the three youths in the burning fiery furnace, while Adam and Christ are portrayed on the side walls. The mosaics were laid over 18 months from June 1902 by George Bridge and his 26 young female assistants from a studio in Oxford Street. The tesserae are of irregular shape and predominantly silver in colour, the effect being toned down by salmon-tinted cement and wide joints. The direct method was the one adopted. In this, full-size coloured drawings (cartoons) of the designs are outlined or traced on to the working surface. The tesserae are then inserted directly into the fixing medium of adhesive cement, using the cartoon as a guide to positioning and colour.

Bentley was not concerned whether the fixing medium was water or oil-based (which allows more time for adjustment before setting), providing it was durable and the tesserae were worked in situ on the walls. In fact oil-based mastic was used. Some sections were prepared in advance – face downwards on canvas in the studio – but the method was judged not to be a success. The advantages of the more traditional direct method are precision, the glittering effect of tesserae inserted individually and thus at different angles to the light, and the difficulty of judging the effectiveness of a mosaic in terms of colour and perspective when it is directly under a bright light (and possibly upside down) in the studio, rather than high on the wall or vault and dimly lit from below.

The direct method was the one used in antiquity, though prefabrication did sometimes occur when working on very detailed designs. One way of doing this is to assemble the tesserae face upwards in a temporary bed of damp sand etc. then cover them with layers of canvas, gauze or strong brown paper pasted with water-soluble gum. Attached to this, the mosaic is lifted from its temporary bed and embedded in a permanent fixing medium on the vault or wall. The paper, gauze or canvas is then soaked with water and removed. Another method in use today in the studio is to glue the tesserae, again face upwards, on to a permanent backing of board, nylon or fibreglass mesh. This is then transferred, in sections if necessary, and secured in the final position with screws or adhesive cement. The reverse method, disliked by Bentley and tried unsuccessfully in the Holy Souls, is to assemble the tesserae face downwards onto gummed, full-size reverse cartoons. When set, the tesserae attached to the cartoons are embedded in the permanent fixing medium on the wall or vault, the cartoons subsequently being soaked with water and removed, to reveal the mosaic (now face up), below. The mosaic is then grouted to produce a level surface.

The reverse method, referred to at the time as 'the modern Italian method' (developed in Venice and Murano in the mid-nineteenth century) was used in the Chapel of St Gregory and St Augustine, across the nave from the Holy Souls. The designer was J R Clayton of Clayton and Bell, famous for its ecclesiastical stained glass. This firm's usual practice, probably also employed here, was to produce full-size reverse cartoons in colour which were then sent to the Venice and Murano Glass Company in Venice for attachment of the tesserae. The young women from George Bridge's studio carried out the mosaic installation work from December 1902 to May 1904, using rectangular, close-jointed, gold tesserae set in mastic with almost geometrical precision. Both here and in the Holy Souls, *opus sectile* – larger pieces of painted glass, cut to shape – was used for the altarpieces. This is because, except when very small tesserae are used, mosaic is less effective to the eye at close range.

Bentley's successor, J A Marshall, designed the next mosaics – the blue and gold flower-like pattern for the lining of the baldacchino (1906) and the simple but effective red and gold decoration of the Shrine of the Sacred Heart, executed by George Bridge's mosaicists in 1911-12 but replaced in 1916, together with the representation of the Holy Face, by James Powell and Sons. The direct method used here was also used for Robert Anning Bell's designs for the altarpiece and blue niche mosaics in the Lady Chapel. Gertrude Martin from George Bridge's studio was the mosaicist here in 1912-13. The same group of mosaicists executed W C Symons' design of St Edmund blessing London in the crypt and the less successful portrayal of St Joan of Arc in the north transept (1910-11). Gertrude Martin returned to the Cathedral in 1922 to put in place more mosaics designed by Anning Bell for the two balconied 'boxes' in the apse.

Basil Cary-Elwes working on the apse mosaics in the Lady Chapel in 1932

Meanwhile the Fourth Marquess of Bute had chosen Robert Weir Schultz, a Byzantine scholar, to organize the decoration of St Andrew's Chapel, which the marquess was funding. The full-size cartoons for Schultz's mosaic designs, in the traditional Byzantine style, were prepared by George Jack. Above the altar and crucifix they show the Cross of St Andrew and his last prayer, while the saint and the story of his life appear on the wall opposite. The side walls show Bethsaida (his birthplace), Constantinople (where he was bishop), Patras (his place of execution), St Andrews in Scotland (which has a relic) and Amalfi and Milan where his remains lie, taken from Constantinople by the Crusaders in 1204. The tesserae were laid in 1913-15 by six of Mr Debenham's mosaicists, including a Venetian, under the direction of Gaetano Meo. The direct method was used. Particularly effective is the glittering vault, with its fish-scale (or cloud) pattern and the birds in the arches.

Cardinal Bourne had chosen Robert Anning Bell to design the first mosaics in the Lady Chapel and the sober tympanum above the main entrance, put up in 1915-16 by James Powell and Sons. But in neither case was he satisfied with the result. He then turned to the artist Gilbert Pownall and established a school of mosaics under Basil Carey-Elwes in the Cathedral tower. From 1930 three English mosaicists, to be joined by two Venetians a year later, used the direct method to execute Pownall's designs in the confessional recess (1930), the sanctuary arch (1932-3), St Peter's Crypt (1934) and the Lady Chapel (1930-5). Work on another design was underway in the vault of the apse when Bourne died in early 1935, but in response to an organized campaign of criticism of Pownall's designs, Bourne's successor, Cardinal Hinsley, agreed to abandon the work and the apse mosaic was subsequently removed.

Twenty years went by before major mosaic work was again undertaken, though a panel depicting St Thérèse of Lisieux by John Trinick was installed in the south transept in 1950 (replaced by the present bronze of the saint in 1958), and another representing Christ the Healer, a memorial to the men of the Royal Army Medical Corps designed and executed by Michael Leigh, went up in St George's Chapel in 1952. Four years later Boris Anrep, who had earlier used the direct method in situ to portray angels above Cardinal Manning's tomb (1914) and St Oliver Plunket in a panel outside St Patrick's Chapel (1924), was commissioned in 1956 to decorate the Blessed Sacrament Chapel.[1] He chose a simple, early Christian style, a pink background and the reverse method. Full-size coloured cartoons were made in his Paris studio, tesserae from Angelo Orsoni selected and attached to the drawings in Venice and the results crated and sent to London. Peter Indri undertook the fixing in 1960-2 but the work was closely monitored and constantly adjusted by Anrep and his assistant, Justin Vulliamy.

Vulliamy also designed the mosaic of St Christopher in the nearby aisle niche but Aelred Bartlett designed and executed that of St Nicholas opposite (1961), together with the mosaic lining the arches between the nave and transepts. Anrep and Vulliamy also worked closely together on the decoration of St Paul's Chapel which followed, but this time Anrep (by now over 80) assisted Vulliamy and designed the principal figures, though in the event he disliked the final result. Again the reverse or indirect method was adopted and Peter Indri did the fixing in 1964-5. Seventeen years later a smaller mosaic went up above the unused north-west entrance door. Designed by Nicolete Gray, it commemorates the 1982 visit of Pope John Paul II and was put in place in June of that year. Translated, the Latin inscription reads 'May this door be the gateway of peace, through Jesus Christ who called himself the gate'.

The mosaicist for the north-west door mosaic was Trevor Caley. In 1999 he returned to install a mosaic panel of St Patrick in its position to the left of St Patrick's Chapel. The predominantly green mosaic was designed and executed by him on board in the studio using unglazed ceramic and traditional glass tesserae from Cathedral stocks, which provide a glittering effect in the light. Two years later another panel was installed. Between St George's and St Joseph's Chapels, it depicts St Alban, an early Romano-British Christian martyr. Around his neck is a red line symbolizing decapitation. Designed by Christopher Hobbs, it was produced in the studio by Tessa Hunkin of Mosaic Workshop and installed by her and Walter Bernadin using the reverse method.

Work is currently in hand to decorate St Joseph's Chapel and plans also exist for the Vaughan Chantry, St George's and two panels in the Holy Souls Chapel. St Joseph's is to have a representation of the Holy Family in the apse above the altar, with a woven gold pattern for the vault and a depiction of craftsmen building the Cathedral on the west wall opposite – a reminder that St Joseph is the patron saint of workers. In an interesting technique, the Holy Family design was projected onto the apse wall and then drawn as a guide to the mosaicist. The designer is again Christopher Hobbs and the mosaicists Mosaic Workshop, who will assemble the tessarae and prepare the mosaics for the apse and west wall on paper in the studio. Once again the reverse or indirect method will be used to produce these but the direct method will be employed on the vault.

[1] For details of the themes and incidents portrayed in the Blessed Sacrament Chapel mosaics, see 'A still point in a turning world' pages 39-41.

A 1950 artist's impression of how the Cathedral will appear when the decoration is finally complete

NOT ANGLES BUT ANGELS

The Chapel of St Gregory and St Augustine tells the story of the evangelization of England from Rome. It starts with the determination of one man, Pope Gregory the Great, to bring this about. It continues with the success of St Augustine and his companions in this mission, then with the subsequent defence of the new faith against both British and foreign non-believers. It concludes with two outstanding leaders of the Catholic Church in England who defended that faith in subsequent dark ages.

The story starts with the panel on the right of the entrance, erected in 1912 and given by the Cathedral Choir School with money raised from performances of a Nativity play. Here is St Gregory the Great, then a Benedictine monk in about the year 587, with three English children in the Roman slave market and remarking 'Not Angles but Angels, if Christian'. It is said that it was then that he conceived the idea of the evangelization of England, an idea brought to fruition ten years later.

Next we move to the altarpiece where Pope Gregory, as he had become, appears with a dove. The story behind this is that his secretary once pulled back a curtain and saw the dove of the Holy Spirit guiding him as he wrote. Beside him in black is another Benedictine, St Augustine, carrying the picture of Christ which he and his companions brought to England, and on either side are some of those companions. They are Saints Paulinus (Bishop of York), Justus (Bishop of Rochester), Mellitus (Bishop of London) and Laurence (successor to Augustine as Archbishop of Canterbury). Both Mellitus and Justus also subsequently held this position.

Up above we have Pope Gregory again, this time enthroned, sending St Augustine and his companions off on their mission, while higher still they are shown meeting Ethelbert, King of Kent, and his Christian wife Bertha. On either side are medallions containing representations of those two great apostles, St Peter and St Paul. Opposite, above the Baptistry arch, is St Augustine together with St John the Baptist, reminding us of the link between baptism and conversion. On each side of them the waters of baptism flow down, while in the archway angels bear the names of the four rivers of Paradise – Euphrates, Gehon, Phison and Tigris.

We move on in time to saints who helped to keep Christianity alive in England after St Augustine and his companions. On the wall facing the entrance are Wilfrid, Bishop of York, and Benedict Biscop, founder of Benedictine monasteries at Wearmouth and Jarrow. Between them they consolidated the link with Rome, a link ratified by the Synod of Whitby in 664. Another seventh-century saint is next – Cuthbert, the 'Apostle to the Lowlands' and later a very reluctant Bishop of Lindisfarne. His evident holiness and humility attracted many northerners to Christianity. He now lies in Durham Cathedral under a slab inscribed simply 'Cuthbertus'. Before the Reformation his body lay in a rich shrine which was the focus of pilgrimage.

If one looks at the head St Cuthbert is carrying, and then at the figure on the opposite wall, one should see the resemblance. St Oswald, Christian King of Northumbria, was slain by the pagan King Penda of Mercia in 642 and carries the red sword of his martyrdom. His head was taken to Lindisfarne Monastery and, when the Danes invaded in 875, hurriedly borne away by the monks in the coffin containing St Cuthbert. At the other end of the entrance wall is another Christian king – St Edmund of East Anglia, killed by Danish archers in 870. Between them the Venerable Bede, father of English history, without whom we would have known almost nothing of the great events occurring in England up to his death in 735.

The chapel was restored in 1996 after damp damage. It was one of the first to be decorated in the Cathedral, from 1902 to 1904. Twenty different marbles from six countries were used, chosen by J F Bentley, who was watching the first go up just before his death in 1902. But the mosaics and the *opus sectile* work were designed by the firm of Clayton and Bell. Unlike the Holy Souls Chapel across the nave, where the mosaic was laid piece by piece, here it was laid in sections. Although put in place by the same team of mosaicists, the style of decoration is very different. J R Clayton believed that any attempt to imitate ancient styles in art was a profound mistake.

A fine example of *opus sectile* is to the left of the entrance. In it King Solomon is shown as the Just Judge. Faced with two women claiming the same baby, so the Bible story goes, Solomon threatened to divide it between them so as to discover the true mother by their reactions. The piece was given by Clayton and Bell as a tribute to Lord Brampton, who donated £8,500 (about £300,000 now) to decorate the chapel. Originally, the judge and his wife were to lie here in a very grand tomb surmounted by effigies. But when they died in 1907 their wills mentioned only a hospital associated with the Cathedral. So that is where the money went.

It seems fitting that the donor should be remembered simply in a panel showing a just judge, a panel given by others. An ornate tomb would be out of place. Only one layman is buried in the Cathedral – Tsar Nicholas II's Ambassador to England – and he had nowhere else to go. Where the Brampton tombs would have gone, a gentle and devout man now lies. Bishop Challoner, Vicar Apostolic of the London District, did much to keep the faith alive when the task seemed hopeless. He died in 1781, just when the tide of intolerance towards English Catholicism was at last turning, leading to Emancipation and the Second Spring. The other tomb in the chapel is that of Cardinal George Basil Hume, Archbishop of Westminster from March 1976 to June 1999. His body lies under a memorial slab of plain white marble in the centre of the chapel – a Benedictine among fellow Benedictines.

THE BLUE ALTARPIECE

There are 33 representations of Our Lady in Westminster Cathedral – carved in limestone and in alabaster, painted on marble and on canvas, cast in metal, and portrayed in many different ways in the mosaics of the Lady Chapel. Almost always Our Lady appears in blue, for this colour, usually the symbol of divine eternity, represents modesty and humility when worn by Our Lady. And it is the blue mosaic altarpiece in the Lady Chapel which must be the most seen and the best loved.

In the altarpiece Our Lady wears a veil and robe of blue and white beneath a green mantle trimmed with gold. She stands facing outwards, a golden halo around her head. Her left hand clasps the hand of the Christ Child whom she supports on her right arm. He is clad in a white robe, a red and gold halo encircling his head and his right hand raised in benediction. The letters MP and OV appear in gold either side – abbreviations of the Greek words for 'Mother of God'. The Latin text around the mosaic reads 'Sub tuum praesidium confugimus sancta Dei genitrix. Nostras deprecationes ne despicias in necessitatibus nostris' ('We flee under your protection, Holy Mother of God. Do not reject our prayers in our hour of need').

The mosaic is enclosed in a frame of statuary marble bearing Our Lady's monogram, crowned and repeated eight times. At the top is a fleur-de-lis, also crowned, symbolizing the Annunciation, while cherubim appear at the springing of the arch. The marble frame was carved by Farmer and Brindley and installed in 1908. The mosaic was designed by Robert Anning Bell, who later designed the mosaic above the main entrance to the Cathedral. The Lady Chapel altarpiece was put in place in 1912 by the mosaicist Gertrude Martin. She also executed the four blue niche mosaics of Old Testament prophets in the Lady Chapel (1912-13) and worked earlier on the mosaics of the Holy Souls Chapel and that of St Gregory and St Augustine. The Lady Chapel altarpiece was donated by a Miss Scott and cost £120 (£5,000 today).

The first Mass in the Cathedral was in the Lady Chapel on the Feast of St Joseph, 19 March 1903.[1] Morning Prayer and Evening Prayer now take place there. During the day baptisms, confirmations, marriages, funerals and memorial services are held in the chapel. Past it go processions on their way to celebrate Mass in the sanctuary, people hurrying to and from the sacristy, the crypt, Cathedral Clergy House and the Choir School. There are also, of course, many who come to the chapel for private prayer, perhaps to say the rosary, and those waiting for Confession who gaze down the chapel at the blue Virgin and Child above the altar and receive reassurance and a blessing.

[1] Not Lady Day, 25 March 1903, as previously believed. See *The Tablet*, 21 March 1903.

I AM THE GATE

The main entrance to the Cathedral consists of central double doors with a smaller door on either side. Above is a huge semicircular arch, deeply recessed, with a span of 40 ft. In the flat semicircular space between this arch and the entrance is the tympanum mosaic. Surprisingly, for such a prominent feature, it was not completed until 1916.

The mosaic itself measures 24ft across and is one of the very few for which J F Bentley produced a design. This formed part of a sketch, in pencil, of the western elevation of the Cathedral and appeared in the *Westminster Cathedral Record* of October 1896. It shows Christ enthroned and displaying his wounds, in a similar fashion to the central figure in the Holy Souls Chapel altarpiece, which Bentley also helped to design. It also recalls the dedication of the Cathedral to the Most Precious Blood. On either side stand the principal saints to whom the Cathedral is dedicated – on the left Our Lady, with St Peter behind her carrying the keys of the Kingdom of Heaven. On the right stands St Joseph carrying a lily, in front of St Edward the Confessor, the first patron saint of England, with crown and sceptre.

Subsequent designs were put forward by Robert Anning Bell, W C Symons (designer of the Holy Souls Chapel), Frank Brangwyn and Professor Seitz, whose radically different design (described in the *Cathedral Record* in December 1900), also related to the dedication of the Cathedral to the Precious Blood. It portrayed a central jewelled Cross with the Divine Pelican – symbol of Christ's sacrifice – superimposed. From the Cross flowed streams of blood and water, with Our Lady and St Peter on either side and harts, sheep and lambs feeding below. In the event there was strong objection to this design (which it was believed could have provoked irreligious mockery) and neither it nor any of the other designs was judged acceptable.

So a return was made to Bentley's original pencilled sketch. After his death in 1902 his assistant John Marshall worked up Bentley's design and provided the colouring. The result appeared in the *Westminster Cathedral Chronicle* in March 1907. The main changes from Bentley's design are that Christ is now fully robed in red and white, with hanging drapery behind the throne. Our Lady is in blue and white, St Joseph in dull red, St Peter in russet and brown and St Edward in purple, white and green, holding the ring he is said to have given to St John the Evangelist. Both St Peter and St Edward are shown kneeling. The background is deep blue with white for the screen running below. The design is generally more sumptuous and contains more accessories than Bentley's simple sketch.

Yet for almost ten years no action was taken. Writing many years later in the *Cathedral Chronicle* of January 1934, Cardinal Bourne confessed that he found the question of the Cathedral mosaics most perplexing, eventually deciding to see for himself great examples elsewhere and seek individual advice from the best sources. For the

Bentley's drawing of the west front of the Cathedral showing the tympanum mosaic

entrance tympanum mosaic he was finally persuaded, most probably by John Marshall, to choose Robert Anning Bell (a Nonconformist). The resulting mosaic he later referred to as 'the greatest disappointment which I have received in connection with the work of the Cathedral'. He believed that Anning Bell had paid little attention to his views and had departed from Bentley's design.

Anning Bell's tympanum mosaic, which we have over the entrance today, is clearly based on Bentley's sketch but there are significant differences. Christ is enthroned, as before, but his wounds are covered and he is blessing with his right hand and holding a book with his left. Inscribed in the book (in Latin) are the words 'I am the gate, if anyone enters by Me he shall be saved' (John 10:9). Thus a new theme is introduced, unrelated to the prominent Latin dedicatory inscription some distance above ('Lord Jesus, King and Redeemer, Save us by Thy Blood'). Except in some of the colouring, the four saints are largely unchanged but, as in Marshall's design, St Peter and St Edward are shown kneeling rather than standing – a consequence of the reduced headroom below the sides of the arch. The background is white and without accessories, not even the screen, and the colours subdued. In general the design is considerably simpler and more austere than those of either Bentley or Marshall.

The tympanum mosaic was completed in March 1916 by James Powell and Sons, using both square and oblong tesserae. The ground in which these were set was grouted level with the surface to ensure durability and prevent frost damage. In April an explanatory article appeared in the *Cathedral Chronicle*. For the most part browns, greys and similar sober colours had been chosen in order to avoid too great a contrast with the surrounding stone and brickwork, with a certain amount of pale red, blue and green to echo the colours of the bricks, sky and any nearby trees. As regards background, it was decided that gold on a flat surface lit by direct sunlight would be unsatisfactory – in contrast with the mosaics over the doors of St Mark's, Venice, where the deeply recessed surfaces are curved and lit by reflected light. Gold tesserae would also be subject to damage from frost and pollution.

A dark blue background had been considered, with considerably lighter figures in the foreground, but the result would have been that any darker shading in the figures would have tended to merge into the background. The effect of years of London smog, grime and acid rain – with steam trains close by at Victoria Station and coal fires in every neighbouring building – would undoubtedly have exacerbated this. So dark figures against a light background had been decided upon, for even if the figures became dimmer and darker as a result of pollution, a definite silhouette would remain and the design as a whole would still be visible. Much thought had also been devoted to the scale of the figures – particularly in relation to the size of the dedicatory inscription above.

Despite this explanation, Cardinal Bourne was unconvinced. He concluded that no non-Catholic could be safely trusted with work of this type or provide the 'inspiration which can be found only in the Catholic faith and in the practice of that faith'. When John Marshall's restraining influence was removed by his death in 1927, Bourne turned to a Catholic artist for something more in tune with his own ideas – something altogether brighter, grander and more ornate. The artist he turned to was Gilbert Pownall.

THE TYMPANUM.

Marshall's design for the entrance tympanum

THE LOST MOSAIC

When Cardinal Vaughan died in June 1903, the great Cathedral which he had founded was essentially complete. But he had left the internal decoration to future generations and it was his successor, Cardinal Bourne, who inherited this responsibility.

Twenty years later the Chapels of the Holy Souls, St Gregory and St Augustine, and St Andrew were complete, as was the Shrine of the Sacred Heart and St Michael. In addition, all the remaining chapels possessed at least a permanent altar and in the sanctuary and elsewhere the marblework was finished. It was a time to take stock and turn once again to the problem of the mosaics.

To commemorate his 20 years as archbishop, Cardinal Bourne had his portrait painted in 1923. He chose Gilbert Pownall, an established Catholic artist, known from his pictures in the Royal Academy. Bourne asked him to prepare mosaic designs – initially for the alcove over the last confessional and then for the Lady Chapel close by. At that time the only mosaics there were those of Our Lady with the Holy Child above the altar and the heads of four prophets who had foretold the Incarnation – all designed by Robert Anning Bell and installed in 1912-13.

The first of Pownall's designs was exhibited in 1927, and in 1930 three mosaicists from the Cathedral, to be joined by two Venetians a year later, started to put the designs into place. Representations of St Peter and St Mary Magdalene over the confessional were rapidly followed by a start on the Lady Chapel apse with its wonderful animal-filled Tree of Life. Work on the Lady Chapel mosaics continued until June 1935.

While the mosaics were going up in the Lady Chapel, in the summer of 1931 Pownall designed the great blue and gold arch mosaic over the sanctuary – Christ enthroned in majesty surrounded by the evangelists, apostles and host of heaven. Two years later the design of the much smaller, and generally praised, arch mosaic in St Peter's Crypt was also ready for the mosaicists. By the end of 1933 they had finished the sanctuary arch mosaic and the following year that in the crypt was complete.

Meanwhile another major work by Pownall was at the design stage. In the summer of 1934 a 3ft coloured cardboard model of a new apse mosaic was exhibited in the crypt. The central symbol was a dove representing the Holy Ghost surrounded by angels. Above the windows were the figures of the apostles and between the windows were scenes from the life of Christ – the Presentation, Agony in the Garden, Crucifixion (centre), Scourging at the Pillar and Crowning with Thorns. At either side were scenes from the Old Testament – Cain and Abel, Moses and the Burning Bush, Pharaoh in the Red Sea and the Tables of the Law.

Work to prepare the great half dome of the apse for the new mosaic started in the autumn of 1934 but by this time criticism of Pownall's style had become intense. It was led by Edward Hutton, a Catholic convert who, five years later,

A photograph of the model of the apse with the suggested design, August 1934

was to design the floor of St Paul's Chapel in a scholarly reflection on the twelfth-century Cosmatesque floor in the Palatine Chapel in Palermo, Sicily.

Hutton's criticisms were expressed at length in a letter which appeared in the *Daily Telegraph* of 7 December 1933. After praising Eric Gill's Stations of the Cross and Robert Anning Bell's blue mosaic altarpiece in the Lady Chapel, he turned to Gilbert Pownall's recent designs. That in the sanctuary of the Lady Chapel, he wrote,

is meaningless, weak and incoherent; the figures are mean and very poorly and clumsily drawn; the drapery ugly; the colour inharmonious and crude. The smaller mosaics in the frieze are confused and 'pretty pretty'. The design, for instance, of the Flight into Egypt is so puerile and unmasterly that it might decorate a commercial Christmas card.

Hutton regarded Pownall's designs everywhere as 'amateurish, clumsy and without mastery and without beauty'. Comparing them, rather unfairly, with the twelfth and thirteenth-century masterpieces in mosaic at Palermo, Monreale, Cefalù and Venice, Hutton found 'poverty, feebleness and vulgarity' in the work at Westminster. As regards the great blue mosaic on the sanctuary arch of the Cathedral, Hutton wrote that 'dismay and grief will not allow me to remain silent. In the empty puerility of its design, the weakness and clumsiness of its drawing and, not least, the ugliness and crudity of its colour, it would seem to involve the whole great church in little less than ruin.'

Clearly irritated, Cardinal Bourne responded in the *Westminster Cathedral Chronicle* of January 1934, defending his choice of artist. He had chosen Pownall with great care and thought and largely approved of the work he had undertaken in the Cathedral. He had decided that what was needed was 'the golden mean between the sixth century mosaics of Ravenna and those installed a thousand years later in St Peter's, Rome'. Neither style, he maintained, seemed suitable for Westminster Cathedral. Above all he wanted the Cathedral to be, not a museum of art, but a house of prayer and that 'everything should assist the piety of the ordinary faithful Catholic'.

Responding to a call in the *Cathedral Chronicle* for moderate and constructive criticism, Hutton offered four suggestions: that plain gold mosaic should cover the walls above the sanctuary, nave and galleries, that any designs for figures should be displayed in situ for at least a year before they were executed in mosaic, that greater care should be taken with iconography and that the mosaics designed by Robert Anning Bell should not be tampered with.

In January 1935 Cardinal Bourne died. Archbishop Hinsley succeeded him in March and Edward Hutton, having failed with Bourne, returned to the attack with his successor. A memorandum to the new archbishop called for work on Pownall's designs to be stopped and for a committee of art experts to be established to advise the Cathedral authorities. The memorandum was signed by the Presidents of the Royal Academy, the Royal Institute of British Architects and the Catholic Art Guild, together with the directors of the National Gallery, the Victoria and Albert Museum and the Courtauld Institute, four members of the Royal Fine Art Commission and others such as Eric Gill. The signatories regarded the sanctuary arch mosaic with dismay and recent mosaic work as 'lacking in the finer qualities of this art'.

Hinsley knew little of mosaics and felt unable to withstand the pressure brought to bear on him. He also privately expressed concern that money which could have been spent on schools was being used for decoration. In November 1935 he ordered that work on the apse mosaic be suspended, Gilbert Pownall being subsequently paid £2,000 in compensation. In 1936 an advisory committee on art, consisting of three laymen and two priests, was established to advise on future projects. The apse mosaic, by then about 20 per cent complete, was subsequently removed altogether. After proposals for a replacement in 1938 (and again in 1954), it was decided to leave the completed sanctuary arch mosaic. Gradually, over the years, this became obscured by gathering dust and grime before at last being cleaned in 1994 in time for the 1995 Centenary – prompting many to believe that it was new.

The 1930s were a time of Art Deco and Modernism, of brave new worlds. It is easy to see how Pownall's pictorial, rather Victorian, style could have grated on both Byzantine purists and 1930s progressives. Yet today his narrative designs, particularly those in the Lady Chapel, must be regarded as among the most popular in the Cathedral. In any event it is sad that a work of art designed for the glory of God and intended to help, in Cardinal Bourne's words, 'the ordinary faithful Catholic', has been lost. For at evening Mass, as the sunlight moves across the blue and gold mosaic on the great sanctuary arch, illuminating Christ amidst the evangelists, apostles and the host of heaven, there are some, at least, who are glad that it's still there – and rather wish the apse mosaic was too.

THE HOST OF HEAVEN AND THE MISSING APOSTLE

When, in October 1933, the sanctuary scaffolding finally came down, after being in place for a year and eight months, it revealed 1,500 sq ft of new mosaic on the sanctuary arch. In the centre was Christ in Glory, surrounded by the four evangelists with six apostles on either side. Three months later, in January 1934, an explanatory diagram appeared in the *Westminster Cathedral Chronicle*. But in the list of the apostles there was no mention of St Matthew. It looked as if someone had blundered.

Christ is shown seated on a rainbow with his feet on the earth. His hand is raised in benediction and he shows the wounds of his crucifixion. The evangelists are represented by an angel (Matthew), a lion (Mark), an ox (Luke) and an eagle (John). Around them are perhaps 1,000 little blue angel faces – the host of heaven – each one formed of mosaic and therefore different. The lining of the lower arch shows seven more angels bearing (in Latin) the gifts of the Holy Spirit: Wisdom, Understanding, Counsel, Fortitude, Knowledge, Piety and Fear of the Lord. The upper arch bears an inscription meaning: 'We believe you are the judge to come. Therefore we beseech you to come to the aid of your servants whom you have redeemed through your precious blood.'

The *Cathedral Chronicle* diagram identifies each apostle by his position in the mosaic rather than by the symbol carried by each one. The group on the left are listed, from the top downwards, as St James the Great (pilgrim's staff), St Peter (keys), St John (chalice and viper), St James the Less (club), St Philip (Roman cross) and St Jude (short lance or arrow). The group on the right are identified as St Matthias (long spear), St Paul (sword), St Bartholomew (knife), St Simon (saw), St Andrew (Greek cross) and St Thomas (set square).

Many of the symbols refer to the apostles' martyrdom. Thus St James the Less is said to have been clubbed, St Paul decapitated with a sword, St Bartholomew flayed alive, St Simon sawn in half and St Andrew crucified on a Greek cross. St James the Great carries the staff of his travels which, according to tradition, took him as far as Spain. Other symbols refer to the poisoned chalice St John was forced to drink (without ill effect) by the high priest at Ephesus, the cross on which St Philip is said to have suffered and which he used to defeat a dragon, the many churches built by St Thomas (patron saint of architects) and, of course, the keys of the Kingdom of Heaven given by Our Lord to St Peter.

But where is St Matthew? There is no mention of him in the list of apostles in the *Cathedral Chronicle*. One explanation could be that he is excluded as an apostle because he already appears in symbolic form in the mosaic as an evangelist. But in that case why does St John appear both as an evangelist and as an apostle? If the number of the apostles is to remain at 12 and St Paul is included, as he often is, then you can't include St Matthias, who was elected by the others to replace Judas (Acts 1:21-6). That, of course, is the most obvious explanation. St Matthias is a mistake for St Matthew. But the figure shown as St Matthias at the top right with a long spear is clearly a very young man – not a very authoritative figure to extract taxes from unwilling Galileans, as St Matthew did as a tax-collector. Indeed St Matthew is portrayed in art as an elderly, dominating sort of man with a long beard. But then so is St Matthias.

The youngest of the apostles were St John, who in the mosaic is just behind St Peter and carries a chalice, and St Jude, the son or younger brother of St James the Less. In art both are usually portrayed as young men, perhaps in their twenties, as St John is here. So could the mystery figure be St Jude? Could the spear be any help in iden-tifying him? Indeed it could. It is in fact one of St Jude's symbols. In the Basilica of St John Lateran in Rome St Jude is shown with a long spear, both in a huge eighteenth-century marble sculpture in the nave and in a smaller seventeenth-century woodcarving.

If the figure listed as St Matthias is really St Jude, then who is the heavily bearded figure at bottom left carrying a short lance or arrow and listed as St Jude in the 1934 *Cathedral Chronicle*? Is St Matthew ever portrayed with a lance? Indeed he is, although an angel or spurned money-bag are much more usual. He can be seen on the Cathedral pulpit with the former and appears in St John Lateran with the latter.

So those looking for St Matthew, patron saint of bankers, accountants and tax-collectors, have a choice. Either a very young man with a long spear at top right, or the heavily bearded figure carrying a short lance at bottom left. But if it's St Jude they are searching for, patron saint of desperate and hopeless situations, then again they must decide. Either top right, clean-shaven, looking very much like the son of St James or, if the bottom left figure is carrying not a lance but an arrow (one of the less common symbols of St Jude), this is the man they need.

IN THE FOOTSTEPS OF ST PAUL

Pope John Paul II's historic visit to Greece, Syria and Malta in May 2001 was a pilgrimage in the footsteps of St Paul whose travels, about 2000 years before, are recorded in mosaic here in his chapel in Westminster Cathedral.

The conversion of Saul (as he was then called), on the road from Jerusalem to Damascus (capital of Syria), is portrayed on the west wall opposite the altar. He has fallen to his knees, struck down and temporarily blinded by a blaze of light. Above is the figure of Christ and below are his words to Saul 'Surge et ingredere civitatem, et ibi dicetur tibi quid te oporteat facere' ('Get up and go into the city and there you will be told what you must do'). Before this experience Saul was a strict Pharisee and ardent persecutor of Christians; afterwards he became a devout Christian himself. Paul's subsequent departure from Damascus is recorded on the wall facing the window. The basket here illustrates his night-time escape down the city wall in a basket, necessary because some of the local Jews were planning to kill him (Acts 9).

On the wall above the windows is another mosaic, this time showing the shipwreck of St Paul off Malta (Melita), when he was under arrest and on his way to trial in Rome. The ship has run aground at a place which is now called St Paul's Bay, and the saint is making his way ashore. Having reached land safely, St Paul was well treated, healing many of the islanders (including the governor's father) of their diseases and being honoured by them accordingly (Acts 27-8).

Having finally reached Rome, St Paul courageously continued his efforts to convert the Gentiles (non-Jews), including many Romans. The final event in his life is commemorated on the wall above the chapel entrance. His execution, in the reign of the Emperor Nero in about AD 64, was just outside the city walls, at a place now known as Trefontane (the Three Fountains). Tradition has it that when his head was cut off it bounced three times and at each place a fountain or spring appeared. Churches were then built above the springs and these are portrayed in the mosaic. Three churches are still there but the springs, while still flowing, are no longer safe to be used for drinking purposes.

The other mosaics in the chapel are the lovely starry blue apse, portrayals of St Peter and St Paul either side of Our Lord on an arch high above the altar, and the great vault (ceiling) mosaic which shows the initial of St Paul together with the palms of martyrdom and the star of David, surrounded by a great tent referring to St Paul's previous trade as a tent maker (Acts 18).

Finally, below the churches of Trefontane and above the Damascus escape basket are a lion and six bees accompanied by the inscription 'De forti egressa est dulcedo' ('Out of the strong came forth sweetness'). This is the riddle of Samson (Judges 14) and here it refers again to the transformation of St Paul from persecutor of the Christians to dedicated Christian evangelist and fearless Apostle to the Gentiles.

At the request of the Cathedral's art committee, the scheme for the mosaic decoration of St Paul's Chapel was initially drawn up in 1961 by Boris Anrep, then working on the mosaics of the Blessed Sacrament Chapel. But Anrep felt too old to take on the responsibility for decorating another chapel and successfully urged that his long-term assistant, Justin Vulliamy, be given the commission – in preference to Aelred Bartlett who had also submitted a scheme for the mosaics of St Paul's.

As with the Blessed Sacrament Chapel, the indirect method was adopted and the mosaic tesserae made and attached to working drawings by the firm of Orsoni in Venice, using full-size coloured cartoons produced by Vulliamy in Paris in 1962-3. The drawings and tesserae were then shipped to London and, after adjustment by Vulliamy, the mosaics were put in place in St Paul's Chapel by Peter Indri in 1964-5. Anrep himself supervised the work and detailed the principal figures in the design, but he was unhappy with the result and subsequently dissociated himself from the project.

ANIMALS AND ANGELS

THOMAS MORE'S MONKEY

The decoration of the Cathedral includes 400 animals – from dragons to dragonflies and lions to ladybirds. There is even a disappearing slug. But it was a monkey, which only made a brief appearance, that caused more controversy and ill-feeling than all the rest put together.

In the summer of 1938, Eric Gill, who had earlier carved the Cathedral Stations of the Cross, was approached by Cardinal Hinsley's advisory committee on art and commissioned to carve an altarpiece for the Chapel of St George and the English Martyrs. It was to be a memorial to Mrs John Boland who founded the CTS Box-Tenders Association and died in 1937. Gill spent three days in October 1938 designing the altarpiece and produced his revised drawings in July 1939. Two of England's most famous Catholic martyrs, Thomas More and John Fisher, had been canonized saints in 1935 and Gill therefore portrayed them gazing up at Our Lord as Priest and King. Both men had been executed by Henry VIII in 1535 for refusing to accept the king as Supreme Head of the Church of England.

Fisher is portrayed as a bishop for he was Bishop of Rochester (and a cardinal). More is shown holding a book inscribed 'Caesaris Caesari et quae sunt Dei Deo' ('To Caesar that are Caesar's and to God that are God's'). But Gill also carved a monkey in the lower left-hand corner. It was explained that

St Thomas had a little zoo of his own at his house in Chelsea and among the inhabitants was a little monkey of whom he was very fond. The sculptor has introduced the little animal as indicating by its very incongruity the deeply human character of the saint – so completely unlike the conventional stained-glass figure. Moreover, the animal does by its caricature of humanity remind us of our lowly state.'

All the essentials, including the monkey, had been carved, but the altarpiece was not quite complete when Gill was forced to stop work in 1940. He died in November following an operation for cancer. The work was finished by his assistant, Laurie Cribb, but remained in Gill's workshop during the war and was put in place in the Cathedral in early 1947. It was when it was revealed to the public that the controversy started – for the monkey had been removed. Although Cardinal Hinsley's art committee had approved the design (including the monkey) in 1938-9, the committee had lapsed with the war and Hinsley had been succeeded by Cardinal Griffin in 1943. Griffin was given a private viewing. He saw the monkey, didn't like it and ordered it to be removed.

Then the storm broke. The *Catholic Herald* received a very large number of letters on the subject, some of them unpublishable. They revealed that no one had been consulted before the Cardinal's decision – neither Mary Gill

(Eric's widow and executor), nor the Cathedral architect, nor even Laurie Cribb, who was putting the finishing touches to the carving in situ. Mary Gill subsequently expressed her consternation, pointing out that the altarpiece had not been fully paid for and she would not have parted with it if its fate in the Cathedral had been known.

Among the first to write to the *Catholic Herald* was Denis Tegetmeier, Gill's son-in-law. He stressed that Gill intended to give the monkey a special symbolic significance. It was an integral part of his conception, not a mere accessory to the saint. David Jones, a close friend and discerning critic of Gill's work, wrote that when the design was executed, the monkey turned out to be one of the more lively parts of the whole work. He explained that Gill 'seemed to be thinking of the ape-ishness in man and, further and more important still, of the whole animal creation, suppliant at the Tree'. Robert Speaight, later Gill's biographer, pointed out that if there was no place for the monkey at Westminster the altarpiece could have been sent elsewhere.

Two letters supported the Cardinal's action. One suggested that a monkey always raises a smile and was therefore inappropriate in a Crucifixion scene. The other was from Fr Arthur Rivers, writing from Westminster Cathedral. He believed that Gill's intention was indeed to portray the 'apeishness of man', for the monkey, 'whilst it possessed the limbs of its kind, had no tail, and its head and torso were those of a boy. It was also to be noted that its arms were raised – apparently in prayer – towards the Figure on the Cross.' He added that the adornment of a church had to be in accordance with the laws of sacred art and with accepted Christian tradition. The monkey would 'have achieved little more than a series of distractions, revolutionary and evolutionary'.

The Administrator of the Cathedral, Canon Howlett, was 84 at the time and the Sub-Administrator, Canon Charles Brown, was 79. The priest actually running things in the Cathedral was the relatively junior Arthur Rivers. Ordained in 1939 and Prefect of the Sacristy at the time he wrote the letter in 1947, the following year he was appointed Cardinal Griffin's Financial Secretary for the Diocese. There seems little doubt that the views in his letter were those of the cardinal.

So what were Eric Gill's intentions in including the monkey? Clearly the first was to show St Thomas More as a human being. Included in More's household at Chelsea were the monkey, two dogs, rabbits, a fox, a ferret, a weasel and an exotic collection of songbirds in an aviary. In the family portrait which More commissioned from Holbein, the monkey and a dog were included. More detested blood sports and liked animals. It was just such human characteristics which appealed to Gill. Indeed his own extended family has been compared with that of More. He was fully conversant with More's masterpiece of humanist philosophy *Utopia*, and prepared the lettering for two editions, including proposals for More's Utopian alphabet. Gill was not the man to portray a plaster saint.

Gill was also reminding us of our own lowliness. Both he and More were essentially humble men. Gill believed there was nothing incongruous in symbolizing mankind in such a way, down on one knee before the Tree of Life. After all, animals have been depicted in churches – Roman, Byzantine and Gothic – throughout history. Indeed the International Society of Sacred Art protested at the removal of the monkey. Animals are also often shown with

Eric Gill working on the altarpiece for the Chapel of St George in his studio

saints. St Francis, who was not above praying with animals, is portrayed with a wide variety, including a wolf. More wrote to Erasmus that he dreamed of being a Franciscan and the order claims him as a Tertiary. Would he have objected to the monkey?

There is a third possible reason for the inclusion. Animals were often used for symbolic purposes in the Renaissance. A monkey was symbolic of the need to avoid worldly temptations. More would have known this and probably so did Gill. But even if the monkey was intended to have such symbolism, and Gill gave no clear indication of this, in the altarpiece St Thomas More's complete attention is devoted to Our Lord on the Cross. The monkey, down on one knee and reaching upwards, is disregarded. If the animal was to be seen as a distraction, then it is being ignored.

A work of art cannot be altered without loss of integrity and impact. The altarpiece has lost an important feature and appears unbalanced. Nothing but a few faint traces of the monkey remain. As for Cardinal Griffin, rightly or wrongly, he has gone down as the man who didn't like animals. But perhaps the final word should come from one of those who wrote to the *Catholic Herald* in February and March 1947. Such a one was Fr Martindale SJ. He wrote: 'Imagine how intrigued children would have been by that monkey! How "real" it would have made St Thomas seem to us! Goodbye lost opportunity!'

(With thanks to John Skelton – Eric Gill's nephew – who, before his death in 1999, gave access to a drawing by Gill of the altarpiece and monkey dated 29 July 1939.)

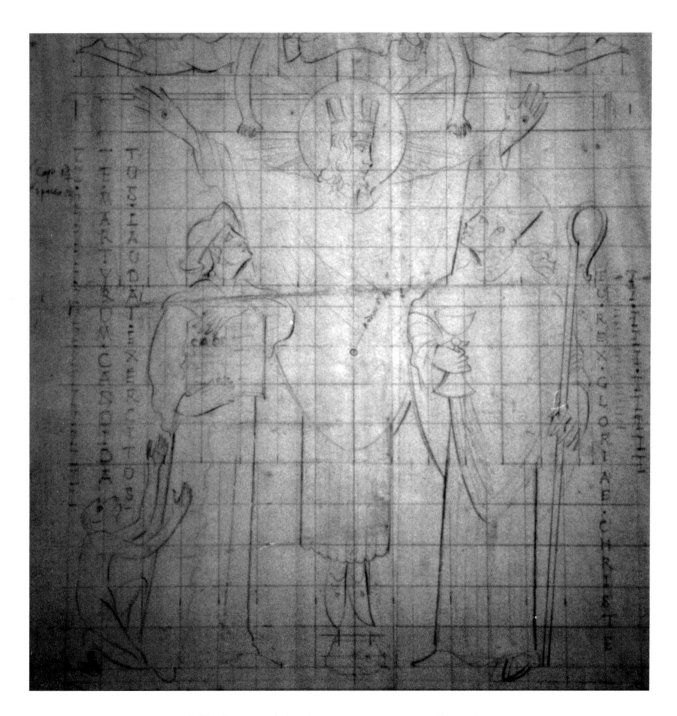

Gill's drawing of the altarpiece – complete with monkey

MAMMALS

When groups of children are shown around Westminster Cathedral they are often given a list of questions. Many of these relate to animals, for there are a surprising number and variety portrayed in the Cathedral.

Starting with the king of beasts first, a winged lion is the emblem of St Mark the Evangelist and this appears at the top of the great 30-ft-high crucifix which hangs above and between the nave and sanctuary. A second is on the left of the blue mosaic on the sanctuary arch, and a third is at the foot of the figure of St Mark on the side of the pulpit. Another lion, wingless and looking decidedly irritable, is on the inner wall of St Paul's Chapel, but this lion relates to the riddle of Samson ('out of the strong came forth sweetness') and refers to the conversion of St Paul. Finally, in St Peter's Crypt the heads of four more lions crown one of the great red granite columns.

St Luke, another of the evangelists, has a winged ox as his emblem; this also appears on the cross, in the blue mosaic and on the pulpit. It is St Luke's Gospel that tells us most about Our Lady and so at the end of the line of pictures which portray her life in the Lady Chapel, there is St Luke busily writing away with a little ox above him. On the other side, and a bit further up, is another ox (no St Luke this time), peering in at the Nativity scene. This includes shepherds and three wise men who have clearly just arrived by camel, two of which are behind them – so maybe they took turns to ride.

Looking in with the ox is, of course, an equally entranced donkey and it, or possibly a relation, is shown a little further on, carrying Jesus and Mary away on their flight to Egypt. A reliable donkey this, sturdy and determined and totally unperturbed by the pagan idols exploding as the Holy Family passes by.

Moving to St Andrew's Chapel, roe deer are to be found either side of the saint here, with sheep above the altar opposite. These appear to be the only sheep in the Cathedral not associated with sacrifice. One should really say 'whole sheep', for there are also 12 marble rams' heads below the cornice in the Lady Chapel and 28 more above the little columns in St Patrick's Chapel. The old Irish regimental badges in this chapel also often bear animals, including a tiger and an elephant but, of course, these do not relate directly to the Cathedral.

Perhaps the nicest animal symbol in the Cathedral is the marble lamb on the front of the pulpit – representing Christ, the Lamb of God. The same symbol appears on the floor of St Joseph's Chapel and in the centre of the vault in the Blessed Sacrament Chapel. As one passes under this chapel's entrance arch, guarded by two archangels, Noah is to the right about to offer up a lamb after the flood, Abel is preparing to do the same on the left and, a little further on, is the ram caught in a thicket which Abraham will also subsequently sacrifice (much to the relief of Isaac).

In a last visit to the Lady Chapel, high up to the right near the entrance is a rabbit standing upright clutching a fir cone. Almost directly opposite on the left is a red squirrel, with another amongst the foliage in a window arch half-way along on the right. These are the two squirrels which children are often asked to find; there are two more in St Joseph's Chapel but these are also traditionally left for visitors to find for themselves.

And finally to St George's Chapel and the missing monkey. As described above, when Eric Gill carved the altarpiece for this chapel in the late 1930s, he included a monkey in the bottom left-hand corner, reaching up towards St Thomas More. But Cardinal Griffin decided that the monkey was too frivolous and ordered it ground out. In any event, looking about 6in below St Thomas More's lower hand, a little white paw emerges, and gradually one is able to follow the monkey's arm downwards until more and more of the animal emerges. So the missing monkey is not entirely missing after all!

BIRDS

There are more birds portrayed in Westminster Cathedral than any other animal. Many of these have symbolic meanings or carry a message but others are…just birds.

To start with there is the eagle, the symbol of St John the Evangelist, the youngest of the apostles. This appears above right in the great blue mosaic on the sanctuary arch, at the base of the 30-ft-high crucifix at the end of the nave and in marble at the foot of the figure of St John on the pulpit.

The Blessed Sacrament Chapel contains a variety of symbolic birds. In a niche on the right before the entrance is a phoenix, said to rise from its own ashes and the symbol of the Resurrection. Opposite is a peacock, symbolizing both immortality and the all-seeing eyes of God. In fact these two birds were often confused which, since the phoenix is a mythical bird and eye-witness accounts therefore rare, is perhaps not surprising. There is another peacock on the floor of St Joseph's Chapel, four more beside the altar in St Paul's, one in the Lady Chapel and eight at the top of one of the little columns supporting the pulpit.

Staying in the Blessed Sacrament Chapel, the next bird is a pelican with three young, this time in gilt bronze at the top of the entrance arch. It is the symbol of sacrifice since the bird was said to feed its offspring with blood from its own breast. The origin of this belief was probably the staining of the pelican's feathers with regurgitated fish. Another pelican is at the top of the tabernacle with two rather plump and well-fed ones in flight above the entrance to the lift.

Probably the most commonly portrayed bird in churches is the dove, since it carries so many messages. In the apse above the altar of the Blessed Sacrament Chapel it symbolizes the Holy Spirit. On the arch dividing the apse from the nave there, the 12 doves are the 12 apostles, while on the right just after the entrance to this chapel is Noah's dove (remarkably like a wood pigeon), carrying an olive branch and symbolizing peace between God and mankind.

The last birds in the Blessed Sacrament Chapel are two hoopoes in a basket, apparently carried by the eldest son, Shem, as Noah and his family leave the ark. While not symbols in themselves, here they represent the survival of all living creatures. Moving up the aisle towards St Joseph's Chapel, St Nicholas, patron saint of mariners, is to be found in a niche on the right accompanied by a wren, the message here being simply that this is a memorial to the wartime head of the WRNS (Women's Royal Naval Service).

St Joseph's Chapel itself has four doves in a basket at the top of the great purple column. These were modelled on those above the priest's entrance in the Byzantine Church of Santa Sophia in Constantinople. The basket shows that they are sacrificial. More doves appear further up the aisle, this time on blue medallions hanging from four electric chandeliers in the Chapel of the Holy Souls, with four more across the nave in the Chapel of St Gregory and St Augustine. These chandeliers may have been modelled on Byzantine jewellery.

BIRDS

St Gregory has his own personal dove – the Holy Spirit of course – whispering into his ear. It is said that his secretary once pulled back a curtain to reveal him receiving divine inspiration in this way. Unfortunately, the doves next door in St Patrick's Chapel are rather more mundane, 28 of them, all with very large feet, at the top of the little columns below the windows.

And so to the aviary in St Andrew's Chapel. The dove high above the altar and crucifix represents the Holy Spirit but there are another 33 message-free birds under the arches. Those above St Andrew resemble pigeons and doves, while those opposite, above the altar, include three kingfishers, two jays, a moorhen and a green woodpecker.

Past St Paul's, and Our Lady's father, St Joachim, is in the niche to the right with a pair of sacrificial doves in a basket. A little further on, the window arch above the confessional is decorated with mosaics of St Peter and St Mary Magdalene, with another dove amidst the green foliage and a cock on the building beside St Peter – a reminder of his thrice denial of Our Lord before the cock crowed.

Another aviary is in the Lady Chapel. On the left is an alert robin above the flower-studded garland which is really a rosary. Moving on, there is a diving swallow and then a blackbird feeding three hungry nestlings. What looks like a lark flies in the arch to the left of Our Lady of Perpetual Succour with two bluetits to her right. Another swallow is above St Dominic with his rosary while below, in the pictures recounting Our Lady's life, is portrayed the Annunciation with the dove of the Holy Spirit swooping down above the angel Gabriel. Two more doves are below the Pietà and a chaffinch perches high up above St John.

Moving into the Lady Chapel apse, as Jesus is presented in the temple, Joseph is behind him carrying a basket with two sacrificial turtledoves. A little later two swallows (the bird of consolation) fly behind him and Mary as they anxiously discover their 12-year-old disputing with the doctors. Either side of the altar are the Old Testament prophets Daniel and Ezechiel, each with two domestic geese. Since both prophets warned of approaching danger, this could be an allusion to the geese of Rome which alerted the sleeping garrison to the approach of the Gauls.

Above the altar in the Lady Chapel the Tree of Life rises above the living water from which a goosander (perhaps) is about to drink. In the tree are a magpie, a blackbird, another black bird with a pink head (which the RSPB guidebook refuses to recognize) and a dove. To the right, the window arch below St Agnes contains two more doves, that below St Lucy has four bluetits with a pair of jackdaws underneath, while just one bluetit appears in the arch below St Justina. In the rosary above the windows are first a swallow, then a wagtail and finally a magpie, while over the passage to the sacristy is a very grand peacock. Finally the coronation of Our Lady on the entrance arch is surmounted by a dove.

The last bird in the Cathedral is on a tree in the crypt, watching St Peter trying to walk on the water. The total is 163, of which at least 44 are symbolic, 18 more carry a message and the rest are…just birds.

INSECTS, REPTILES AND FISH

Having already described the mammals and birds portrayed in the Cathedral, we can now deal with the other living creatures to be found there. Starting with insects, there are six rather nice bees on the inner wall of St Paul's Chapel relating (like the lion described earlier) to the riddle of Samson and referring to St Paul's conversion. Moving down to the Lady Chapel, there are three more bees and a beehive high on the left just inside, in amongst the flower garland which is really a rosary. Nearby is another insect which might be another bee but looks more like a flying ant and will therefore be listed as a UFI (unidentified flying insect).

Moving along the rosary there is another UFI (perhaps a wasp), followed by a beetle. After the blackbird's nest is a cabbage white butterfly, then our third UFI, another beetle and finally a red admiral butterfly. Going past the chapel apse and continuing along the rosary on the south or right wall, there is a definite wasp, a ladybird, another UFI, a blue butterfly (perhaps a holly blue) with five more in the arch below St Agatha, a dragonfly, a mauve butterfly, a fifth UFI and finally a ladybird to the right of the entrance.

Back now to the apse of the Lady Chapel with its wonderful Tree of Life, and contained within its branches an amazing variety of insects. Five butterflies (a peacock, two cabbage whites, a tortoiseshell and a red admiral) are to be found, together with a grasshopper, a stag beetle, a dragonfly, a caterpillar, four ladybirds and another three UFIs. Gilbert Pownall, who designed this mosaic in the 1920s, filled his notebooks with pictures of English insects and birds. The results are to be seen here.

And so to the story of the disappearing slug. Two to three feet above and to the right of the head of Christ on the Tree of Life is a bird with a black body and pink head. After completion in 1932 dust, dirt and candle smoke caused the pink head to blend in with the surrounding gold mosaic. As a result all that could be seen was a small black form, closely resembling a slug, described by one priest (Canon Francis Bartlett) to visitors as 'surely the least attractive of God's creatures'. Only periodic cleaning of the mosaic (most recently in 1993) revealed the slug to be in fact a bird.

From insects to reptiles and down to the crypt for the first dragon. And there it is at the foot of the effigy of Cardinal Wiseman, first Archbishop of Westminster, with his crosier firmly thrust into its mouth. Dragon-watchers will notice that this is a wingless and therefore probably immature specimen. But above, in the little Chapel of the Sacred Heart and St Michael, the archangel can be seen vanquishing a winged and savage adult. There are two more dragons, though rather difficult to find, on the underside of the great sanctuary arch.

From dragons to serpents and snakes, all of which symbolize evil. On the inner wall of the Chapel of the Holy Souls is the serpent in the Garden of Eden coiled around Adam, with the skull of death in its jaws. Opposite, the same serpent is crushed underfoot by Christ. Crossing the nave to St Patrick's Chapel there are eight snakes

Fish on the floor of St Andrew's Chapel

decorating the altar and 48 more at the top of the Cork red columns below the windows – 32 of them with gaping jaws and lots of teeth. Tradition has it that St Patrick expelled the snakes (and thus evil) from Ireland, cleverly persuading the last to get into a box (to see if it would fit) before slamming the lid and throwing it into the sea.

Moving down to the Lady Chapel, above the altar Our Lady can be seen crushing another serpent, as Christ is doing in the Holy Souls Chapel, while down in St Peter's Crypt are the last snakes, eight of them in pairs, decorating the top of one of the great red granite columns. And it is here in the crypt mosaic that the first fish are portrayed – a dolphin and a young swordfish in medallions and another dolphin, which can only be described as snarling, in the sea. Why the ill humour, one wonders.

Returning to the Lady Chapel, the vines around the rosary are emerging from the mouths of 11 fish. One should really say 'fishlike creatures' since they are all mouths and ears and very little else. Across in the apse of the Blessed Sacrament Chapel two fish are shown at the Feeding of the Five Thousand while under the three windows on the left are two more fish with the Greek word for fish (ΙΧΘΥΣ) between them. This word is made up of the initial letters of the phrase 'Jesus Christ, Son of God, Saviour'. So a fish was a symbol for Christ.

A fish also appears on the floor of St Joseph's Chapel and, though not easy to see, another is in a pool in the mosaic at the entrance to St George's. But it is in St Andrew's Chapel across the nave that fish really hold sway. St Andrew, like his brother St Peter, was of course a fisherman and there are 29 fish and other marine creatures amidst the waves on the floor, including a swordfish, cod, skate, sole, plaice, salmon, rays, eels, a rather nice lobster, two crabs, a starfish, anemone, whelk and scallop.

Adding them all together, there are 45 insects, 71 reptiles and 49 fish in the Cathedral. As described earlier, there are also 72 mammals and 163 birds, altogether making up a total of exactly 400 living creatures. Plus, of course, one disappearing slug and one missing (but not quite) monkey.

One final word. When children are taken around the Cathedral they can be a bit noisy. They often have questionnaires to fill in and need to ask questions. But they do try to keep quiet near the Blessed Sacrament Chapel and the confessionals where people are praying. And happy, interested children will want to come back, with their parents and then with their children and perhaps one day with their children's children. One excited six-year-old little boy once ran over and said 'this is the bestest, bestest church I've ever been in'. One cannot ask for anything more.

BETWEEN HEAVEN AND EARTH

Angels are spiritual beings, messengers and servants of God, able to bridge the gulf between heaven and earth, and they are portrayed many times, and in many different ways, in the Cathedral. The word is derived from 'aggelos' meaning messenger in Greek. They were first represented in fourth-century Byzantine art and by the late fifth century Christians had decided that there were nine types (choirs) of angels arranged into three groups of three - thus reflecting the Holy Trinity. First are Seraphim, described by Isaiah as leading the divine worship from around the throne of God. They are shown in art as human heads with six wings - the absence of a body emphasizing their spiritual nature. At Westminster Cathedral artistic representations appear in the Holy Souls and Lady Chapels and in the crypt above the tomb of Cardinal Manning.

Next are Cherubim, left to guard the Tree of Life in Eden after the Fall. Other Old Testament references confirm that they are protectors of sacred objects such as the Ark of the Covenant. Ezechiel describes Cherubim carrying the throne of God in flight and they are often shown as winged heads of little boys. It is appropriate that representations should be found in the Blessed Sacrament Chapel of the Cathedral - with uplifted wings either side of the throne behind the tabernacle and also as winged heads at the six corners of the canopy above the altar and on the entrance and side grilles - 90 Cherubim in all.

We know almost nothing about the next five choirs of angels, briefly referred to by St Paul in his letters to the Ephesians and Colossians. The early Christians decided that Thrones, like Seraphim and Cherubim in the same group, are dedicated to the contemplation and adoration of God, while the second group - Dominions, Virtues and Powers - govern the universe. In the subordinate group, Principalities are said to be the guardians of nations and sovereigns while only the last two choirs - Archangels and Angels - reveal the divine plan to mankind and assist ordinary mortals.

Of the Archangels, we know quite a lot about Michael, Gabriel and Raphael, who reveals to young Tobias that there are, in fact, seven Archangels in all. Michael is the leader of the heavenly hosts and the angel of judgement who, as described in the Apocalypse, defeats Satan and his fallen angels in heaven and casts them down to earth. With Gabriel he guards the entrance to the Blessed Sacrament Chapel and he also appears in the Holy Souls and Lady Chapels in the Cathedral. But for some he is shown most effectively subduing a dragon on the altar frontal of the little Shrine of the Sacred Heart.

The name Gabriel means messenger and he is, of course, best known as the heavenly messenger to Our Lady to announce the forthcoming birth of her son, Jesus, as portrayed in the Lady Chapel. About six months earlier Gabriel had told Zechariah that he too would have a son - John the Baptist. In the Old Testament Gabriel is sent to Daniel to tell him of Christ's future incarnation and interpret his visions. He is usually shown carrying the lily of the Annunciation, as he is in the apse of the Lady Chapel.

The third Archangel is Raphael, which means 'God heals', and we know a good deal about him as well. In response to prayer, he is sent by God just as Tobias is about to set off on a dangerous journey. Disguised as a young man he acts as his guide and protector, subdues an evil spirit, arranges a successful marriage for Tobias and cures his father of blindness – apparently resulting from cataracts. It is only after his mission is fulfilled that he reveals his true identity. In the Cathedral he is shown to the left of St Michael in the Chapel of the Holy Souls.

Other, unnamed, angels appear frequently in the Old Testament, as messengers, guides, protectors and interpreters of God's will. Jacob's vision shows them using a ladder to move between heaven and earth. The mosaics in the Blessed Sacrament Chapel show some of their activities, including preventing Abraham killing Isaac, protecting the three young men in the burning fiery furnace and persuading the weary Elijah to eat. Elsewhere in the Cathedral they can be seen bearing divine messages – the seven spiritual and corporal works of mercy in the Holy Souls Chapel and the seven gifts of the Holy Spirit on the sanctuary arch.

In the New Testament, angels announce Christ's incarnation and birth, minister to him when tempted in the desert, strengthen him in the agony in the garden, roll away the stone from the tomb and explain his Resurrection and Ascension to his disciples. An angel later rescues St Peter from prison and in the Apocalypse we learn how angels will vanquish Satan and his followers, accompany the Last Judgement and convey the souls of the righteous to heaven. In the Cathedral, angels are shown supporting Christ's cross in St George's Chapel and receiving his blood in a chalice at the Twelfth Station of the Cross, sounding trumpets below the organ screen and as a myriad little blue faces surrounding Christ in Glory on the sanctuary arch.

And so to those angels to whom God has given the task of protecting us during our time on earth, angels so close to us that they may call us brothers – guardian angels. St Thomas Aquinas believed that only angels of the lowest order are given this task, those perhaps who understand us best, while other saints believed that sin can drive them away. In St Matthew's Gospel, Jesus speaks of children having angels in heaven who are continually in the presence of his Father. It is comforting to think that we have each been given the protection of a guardian angel – those watchers and holy ones of God – unable to rest until we have passed safely from this world through death and judgement to the next.

How many angels are there and how do we recognize them? Myriads of myriads according to the Book of the Apocalypse. As to appearance we can never be sure, for they are divine spirits rarely visible to us, and then perhaps only indistinctly as grey protectors. Raphael is described by Tobias as a gracious young man and the early Christians thought of angels in the same way. Only in the fourth and fifth centuries did they begin to be portrayed with wings and haloes. Interestingly, the angel seen only 85 years ago by the children of Fatima (a youth of about 14 dressed in white) sounds very like both Gospel descriptions and very early Christian representations. But the Bible makes clear, and it is wise to remember, that angels do not always look like angels.

MEMORIALS AND MARTYRS

ST JOHN SOUTHWORTH: THE STORY OF THE BODY

John Southworth, parish priest of Westminster, was hanged, drawn and quartered at Tyburn (near Marble Arch) on 28 June 1654. His only offence was to be a Catholic priest, which he freely admitted. His body now lies in St George's Chapel in Westminster Cathedral, close to where he lived and worked. But in between there lies a journey, shrouded in secrecy, which covered some 400 miles and took 275 years.

John Southworth was arrested in his bed on 19 June, sentenced on the 26th and executed two days later. Among thousands of spectators was the Venetian Secretary to England. He records that, after the rope had been put around Southworth's neck and the cart drawn away, 'in a fashion worse than barbarous, when he was only half-dead, the executioner cut out his heart and entrails and threw them into the fire kindled for this purpose, the body being quartered, one for each of the quarters of the city'. But the Venetian's last supposition was to be proved wrong.

Someone with inside knowledge was Richard Symonds, a Royalist and antiquarian. He confided to his note-book that the Spanish Ambassador had bought the body from the executioner for 40 shillings (about £2,000 today). This would have been made easier by the fact that there were up to 12 other prisoners executed at Tyburn that day – including five coiners who suffered the same treatment for treason as John Southworth. A faded piece of paper identifying a relic relates what happened next. It refers to 'Mr James Clark, surgeon, who embalmed the body'. Both the Royal College of Physicians and Cambridge University record a James Clarke (or Clerke) who was awarded his medical doctorate in 1656-7.

On 5 June 1655, George Leyburn, President of the English College of Douay (Douai, near Lille), reported that Southworth's body had been sent there by two English Catholics of the highest rank. Leyburn had known Southworth well for many years in London. Bishop Richard Challoner later confirmed the arrival. Challoner was at Douay for 25 years from 1705. He was thus able to study the records and perhaps speak to those alive in 1655. He writes that 'Mr Southworth's body was sent over to the English College of Douay by one of the illustrious family of the Howards of Norfolk, and deposited in the church near St Augustine's altar.'

Almost certainly it was Philip Howard, third son and later Cardinal Protector of England, who organized the body's embalming and despatch to Douay. To the dismay of his family he had become a Dominican. Letters from him of September 1654 and October 1655 to the master-general of his order show that he was in England 'on urgent business'. His father was dead, his eldest brother Thomas (later 5th Duke of Norfolk) was mentally ill in Padua and Henry, the second son (later 6th Duke), was occupied with family affairs and possibly also abroad. Three of Philip's younger brothers had arrived to study at Douay in 1653 and in 1656 one of them, Francis (then

16), was given up for dead by his doctors, but made a miraculous recovery after prayers were offered to John Southworth and flowers and a pillow from his head brought to the youth.

Such was the devotion of the people of Douai at Southworth's shrine and the benefits reported to have been received that Leyburn was forced 'to mitigate the veneration and public concourse of people' – presumably by removing the body from public view. In this he was obeying a decree of Pope Urban VIII on the veneration of martyrs. It was not until 1741 that relics of the Douay martyrs were allowed to be placed in altars and after this Southworth's body, in a leaden coffin, was placed under the altar table of St Augustine, about half-way down and probably on the left-hand side of the church. There it remained until 1793.

England and France went to war in January 1793. The National Guard arrived at the college, seals were set on objects and rooms and three guards (known as 'the three spiders') were posted. Despite this, much valuable property was spirited away and buried by students while the relics, including the hair-shirt of St Thomas of Canterbury, the biretta of St Charles Borromeo and the body of John Southworth, were buried by the priests. It is fortunate that two records were left. Bishop Douglass wrote 'Mr Southworth's body in the Kilns exactly in the middle – six feet deep'. Father Thomas Stout, who seems to have been responsible for the relics, went one better and left a plan showing their position in the malt-kilns (used for beer-making). Later that year, in August 1793, the English were expelled from the college.

Not until 1863 was there a search for the buried objects. Some table silver was found near the refectory but nothing else. Sixty years later, in 1923, the town council of Douai decided to build a new road to the railway station where the old college had been. In 1926 the site was cleared, the road built and the surrounding land sold. In July 1927 workmen began to dig a cellar, the only one planned, for a shop at the corner of Rue Durutte and the new road (now Avenue Clemenceau). On the 15th a pick struck a leaden coffin 5ft 8in long, moulded to the shape of a human body with the head towards the south-east. A hole, about $1\frac{1}{2}$ in across, was in the centre. The authorities were notified, a priest (Albert Purdie) summoned from England and the coffin, which was in two halves, the upper fitting tightly over the lower, was opened.

Inside lay the body of a man swathed in brown linen bandages. These had been treated with preservative and were very strong. Water penetrating through the hole (almost certainly caused by a metal probe used in the 1863 search) had badly damaged the chest and stomach but the head, which bore a slight moustache and beard, was well preserved and had been roughly severed from the trunk. The hands, ears and crown of the head were missing (presumably taken as relics). The brain and the internal organs had been removed and carefully replaced with preservative material. No expense had been spared in embalming the body in accordance with a method described in 1629. Subsequent X-ray results confirmed that the body had first been quartered and then meticulously sewn together.

The day after the discovery of the body a workman found a wooden box some 8ft away. Inside were the remains of the relics of St Thomas Becket and St Charles Borromeo. Comparison of the position of this box and the coffin with Fr Stout's plan confirmed that the body was that of John Southworth. The complete absence of any identifying marks suggests that this simple leaden coffin may have been used to carry the body from England in 1655, when anonymity was essential. Tape binding the coffin, reported in 1786, indicates that it was normally kept closed but could be opened when necessary – as when Francis Howard was close to death.

In December 1927 John Southworth came back to England, his right forearm and left clavicle remaining as memorials in Douai. From Dover the body travelled to St Edmund's College, Ware, lineal descendent of Douay College. In April 1930 it returned to London, first to Tyburn Convent, and then, on 1 May, accompanied by a great procession, to St George's Chapel in Westminster Cathedral. In late 1954 the body was clothed in vestments in the style of his time, a silver mask and hands added, and the martyred priest revealed to the public gaze.

There St John Southworth now lies, canonized a saint in 1970, in death his face curiously unlined beneath the silver mask, despite his 35 years as a Catholic priest in a hostile land. Perhaps he even crossed this spot as he ministered to the poor and plague-stricken of Westminster, walking the green fields between the Bridewell prison, now the Army and Navy Stores, and 'the Five Houses', an isolation hospital for plague victims, at a place now close to Vauxhall Bridge Road.

THE RUSSIAN IN THE CRYPT

Westminster Cathedral is not known for its tombs. There are only ten, one of which (Cardinal Vaughan's) is not a tomb at all – but a monument with a sculpted effigy of the man. The founder of the Cathedral wished to be buried in another of his great foundations, the Missionary College at Mill Hill. Seven other Cardinal Archbishops of Westminster and the great Bishop Challoner, who led the Catholic Church in England for a large part of the eighteenth century, are interred in the Cathedral. The tenth sepulchre is that of a layman with no role in the Diocese of Westminster. And thereby hangs a tale…

Count Alexander Benckendorff was born in the Baltic provinces of Russia in 1849, his mother being a princess. He was educated in France and Germany, then served as a diplomat in Rome, Vienna and Copenhagen. Finally, from 1903 until his death he was Russian Ambassador to England. An anglophile, in 1911 his only daughter married the second son of an English viscount, the Hon Jasper Ridley. Count Benckendorff encouraged the teaching of Russian at British universities and was Honorary President of the newly formed Russo-British Chamber of Commerce. Unusually for a Russian, he was a Roman Catholic.

With 1914 came the Great War. Russia, allied with Britain and France, suffered a series of crushing defeats. By 1917 war-weariness, antagonism towards the Tsar's family (the Tsarina in particular) and the allure of revolutionary socialism, brought Russia close to collapse. By March, Tsar Nicholas II had offered to abdicate, intending to spend the rest of the war abroad and then to settle quietly in the Crimea where he would devote his life to the education of Aleksei, his haemophiliac son. Instead he was placed under house arrest and in July 1918, on the orders of the Bolshevik Urals Soviet, he and his family were shot.

Meanwhile a severe influenza epidemic was sweeping Europe. Count Benckendorff, the Tsar's ambassador to the Court of St James's, was one of the first to be struck down. On 8 January 1917 he took to his bed. Three days later the condition had congested his lungs and he died. Before his death he told his daughter, by now the Hon Mrs Jasper Ridley, of his earnest wish to be buried in Westminster Cathedral where he had worshipped regularly. This wish she conveyed, not only to the Cathedral but also to the British government.

The only people buried in the Cathedral at the time were the first two Archbishops of Westminster, Cardinals Wiseman and Manning. Their remains had been transferred to the crypt in 1907 from an initial place of rest in Kensal Green Cemetery. Cardinal Bourne, the fourth Archbishop of Westminster, had left for Rome in December 1916 and did not return until April 1917. Communications between London and Rome had to pass through several war-torn countries. Letters could take a week to arrive and telegrams two days. Meanwhile in Russia the Imperial Family was in turmoil, and communications subject to strike action. With these difficulties, together with the fact that the Count had died at 10pm on a Thursday, *The Times* reported on Monday that 'to the request that the body might be interred in the Cathedral, no reply has been received from Cardinal Bourne'.

On Saturday, 13 January 1917, a private memorial service was held for members of the count's family and staff at the Russian Embassy. On Sunday the body was brought to the Cathedral to lie overnight before the high altar under the Russian flag, prior to a Solemn Requiem Mass the following day. Count Benckendorff's Requiem Mass must have been one of the most unusual in the Cathedral. On a cold, gloomy winter's day, a guard of honour of Grenadiers, together with the band of the Irish Guards, was drawn up outside. Within the Cathedral the coffin lay before the sanctuary steps covered with a black pall and white cloth embroidered with the imperial arms of Russia. On a cushion at the foot lay Count Benckendorff's medals and other decorations. On each side of the coffin stood three tall candles. A few paces from each, a British soldier leaned on his reversed rifle while an officer stood at the foot of the coffin.

Despite the problems of arranging the Requiem Mass at short notice during a weekend in wartime, members of both the British and Russian royal families attended. King George V was represented by the Duke of Connaught, the Tsar by his brother, the Grand Duke Michael. The Grand Duchess George of Russia was also present and the Queen, the Prince of Wales and five royal princesses sent representatives. Mrs Lloyd George (wife of the Prime Minister) was there and Cabinet members included Mr and Mrs Asquith, Mr Balfour, Mr Austen Chamberlain, Lord Robert Cecil, Lord Curzon, Lord Derby and Lord Milner. A week later, on Monday 22 January 1917, Count Benckendorff's wish was granted.

He was buried in the crypt of Westminster Cathedral where he had been a constant worshipper during the last 14 years of his life. At this simple service his wife, too distressed to attend earlier ceremonies, was the chief mourner, together with the daughter who had played such a key role in bringing the Count to his last resting place. It was the Count's daughter who also commissioned Eric Gill (then working on the Cathedral Stations of the Cross) to produce the memorial slab which lies above the ambassador's tomb in the crypt. It was finally installed early in 1939. In Russian and Latin, the inscription reads: 'Count Alexander Philip Constantin Ludwig Benckendorff, Ambassador Extraordinary and Plenipotentiary for Russia to the Court of St James's. August 1 1849 – Jan 11 1917. Requiescat in Pace.'

Cardinal Bourne must have been under considerable government pressure to agree to the interment in the Cathedral. Russia was a military ally and its seemingly imminent collapse would release many German divisions to fight Britain and France on the Western Front. It was a time to show solidarity with Russia, not for a snub, real or imagined. The Count's daughter knew what she was doing when she publicly declared her father's wish to the British government. Soviet Russia has passed into history as did the Russia of the Tsars and an era of religious and political freedom has dawned in Eastern Europe. In 1991 the first post-Soviet Russian Ambassador since Count Benckendorff was appointed to the Court of St James's.

OUR LADY OF VILNA

On the left of the entrance to the Lady Chapel is a gate of wrought metal. It leads along a passage past the main sanctuary to the sacristy, crypt and Long Corridor, which in turn leads to Clergy House. Above the gate is a circular medallion in gilt metal with a relief of the Virgin and Child. The image is that of Our Lady of Ostra Brama, Our Lady of Vilna.

The medallion was presented by the Polish fighter squadron, City of Vilna, on 15 March 1944. The Latin inscription reads (in translation) 'In the name of the Polish Air Force, the Reconnaissance Squadron of Vilna dedicates this offering to you, most blessed Mother, entreating you to restore Vilna when, ever vigilant, you bestow your favour upon the destiny of the homeland'.

The city of Vilna, or Vilnius as it is known today, lies where the river Vilnia flows into the river Neris amidst picturesque, pine-clad hills. The tenth-century city contains numerous old Catholic churches, including a fourteenth-century cathedral. The revered image of Our Lady of Vilna, long an object of pilgrimage, is in a shrine above an ancient gate known to Lithuanians as Ausros Vartai (the Gate of Dawn) and to Poles as Ostra Brama (the Pointed Gate) – the last remnant of the city walls built between 1503 and 1552.

Although suffering temporary occupation by Russia (1655-60), Sweden (1702 and 1706) and France (1812), for over 400 years from 1323 Vilnius was the capital of the Grand Duchy of Lithuania, before being ceded to Russia in 1795. After World War I, the city was occupied by both Lithuania and Russia before being annexed by Poland in 1920. In 1939 it was occupied by Soviet troops following the partition of Poland, and ceded back to Lithuania as its capital. Vilnius became the capital of an independent Lithuania in 1991 and Poland formally renounced any claim to the city in the Friendship and Co-operation Treaty of 1994.

The other Polish memorial in the Cathedral commemorates the members of the Polish armed forces who died in World War II and was installed in 1965. It is to the left of the altar in St George's Chapel. An appropriate place, for the Poles fought heroically for freedom alongside the British, and alongside the Polish memorial, either side of Philip Lindsey Clarke's 1931 carving of St George, are the names of some of the British and Commonwealth Catholic servicemen who died in war.

PER ARDUA AD ASTRA

The most unusual memorial in the Cathedral must be the Chi-Rho (the first letters of Christ's name in Greek) made of thousands of nails between the confessionals in the south transept. It commemorates the men of the Canadian Air Force who died in World War II.

The first Canadian memorial, completed in 1947 and dedicated in October 1948, consisted of an altar in the Baptistry in honour of St Anne, Our Lady's mother and Canada's Patron Saint. The altar, funded by £1,000 raised for the purpose, was set against the west wall below the windows and was clad with ornamental marble with a central cross on the frontal.

In 1967, Winefride de l'Hôpital, biographer and eldest daughter of the Cathedral architect, J F Bentley, died. Both she and an unmarried sister, Miss H M Bentley, who also died at about this time, left bequests for the further decoration of the Cathedral. It was decided to use the money to complete the marble revetment of the Baptistry and work started in 1969. With Canadian approval it was also decided to remove the Baptistry altar and transfer the dedication to a new marble altar facing the congregation in the centre of the Blessed Sacrament Chapel.

These decisions were taken in the light of the changes introduced by the Second Vatican Council (1962-5), one of which was that the celebrant should face the congregation during the Mass. However, a permanent new altar in the centre of the Blessed Sacrament Chapel would have radically altered the appearance of the chapel and obscured the fine marble floor. The temporary altars introduced after Vatican II for use in the Cathedral are on aluminium frames, and so can be removed when not required.

When the scheme for the new memorial altar was abandoned, the next plan was for a plaque in the south transept. The man chosen to design it was David 'Birdie' Partridge, a naturalized Canadian born in Ohio in 1919. After serving in the Canadian Air Force as a flying instructor in 1942-5, Partridge took up as a painter and printmaker. In 1958 he produced his first three-dimensional sculpture comprising different sized nails; he developed and perfected this technique during his ten years in London from 1962. He was deeply influenced by early studies of geology and palaeontology and by hours of flying over Northern Ontario during the war, and this is reflected in his works now to be seen in galleries in Canada, Australia and the USA. His 'Vertebrate Configuration' is in the Tate Gallery, London.

The current Canadian Air Force memorial in the south transept of the Cathedral was installed in 1972. It takes the form of a Chi-Rho in thousands of shining nails of many different lengths. The central 'X' may also be viewed as commemorating the runways of a wartime airfield and the triple circle as the roundels or 'bull's-eye' markings on Canadian aircraft. The nails themselves may be taken to symbolize the 17,101 members of the Royal Canadian Air Force who never returned from the war.

The inscription below the memorial is by Edward Wright. It reads: 'To the Glory of God and in cherished memory of their beloved comrades this panel is erected by the Catholics of the Royal Canadian Air Force overseas. RIP' Above it, on 1 July each year, when we commemorate the dedication of the Cathedral, a single candle burns.

And St Anne, Patron Saint of Canada? With her husband, St Joachim, they appear on either side – in the niches at the near end of the south aisle and in the first little mosaic tableau on the left of the Lady Chapel.

ALONG THE WAY

High on a massive pier opposite the Canadian Air Force memorial is a bronze sculpture in low relief. It shows a nun hurrying along but glancing back as she goes. It is a representation of St Thérèse of Lisieux, St Teresa of the Child Jesus, whose 'Little Way' of achieving perfection in small, everyday things is the heart of her spirituality.

The simple, almost austere, bronze is by Manzù, one of Italy's best known post-war sculptors, and was made in Milan. Installed in 1958, it replaced a 1950 mosaic representation of the saint by John Trinick. Earlier Trinick had been responsible for the lovely portrayal of Our Lady of Walsingham in *opus sectile* on the side of the present pulpit, erected in 1934.

Giacomo Manzù was born to a poor family in Bergamo in 1908. He started work at 13 as a gilder and stuccoist. In 1929 he was commissioned to decorate his first chapel and was producing naturalistic bronze sculptures by 1934. Always fiercely anti-Fascist he had become a Marxist by the end of World War II. Yet he continued to portray religious themes, sometimes introducing elements reflecting contemporary violence. A bronze portrayal of a plump cardinal, dating from 1947-8, can be found in the Tate Gallery, London.

In 1947 Manzù entered a competition to design the new bronze door at the entrance to St Peter's Basilica, Rome. He persuaded Pope John XXIII, who came from the same home town, to agree to a bronze Door of Death, representing the threshold to another world. This door, on the left of the enormous entrance, was produced in 1964-7. Mainly concerned with the deaths of saints, it included at its base a row of animals and birds (squirrel, hedgehog, owl, etc.) which Manzù must have particularly enjoyed sculpting. He died in 1991.

The bronze of St Thérèse is on an aisle which many people pass along as they go to and from the sacristy and Clergy House. It is indeed 'along the way'. Yet the position is a quiet one too, as people sit nearby preparing for confession. Why is it so effective? Perhaps because it shows the saint who founded the 'Little Way' as she was in life – humble, simple and devout. Where is she hurrying and to whom does she turn as she goes? Perhaps she is travelling the way she herself found to Heaven – 'a new way, very short, very straight, a little path'. Yet despite her haste she has time to look back, with what appears to be compassion.

ST VINCENT AND ST BENEDICT

Either side of the Canadian Air Force memorial are bronze reliefs of two saints whose lives and work provide the inspiration for organizations today – St Vincent de Paul and St Benedict of Nursia. Both bronzes were executed by Bryan Neale RA and unveiled in 1998 and 1999 respectively.

St Vincent de Paul was born into a peasant farming family in Gascony in 1581 and died in Paris in 1660. Ordained a priest in 1600, he was initially satisfied with serving as a chaplain to rich and influential families. But by 1617 he had resolved to devote his life to caring for the poor, the homeless, the sick and elderly, and for children abandoned by their parents – in a word, the dispossessed. For him 'the service of the poor is to be preferred to all else, and to be performed without delay'. During his lifetime his work spread to more than ten countries. Today it continues to be carried on by the priests of the Congregation of the Mission (known also as Vincentians and Lazarists), and by the Daughters (or Sisters) of Charity and the laymen of the Society of St Vincent de Paul (founded 1833), who both work in the Cathedral parish.

The memorial in the Cathedral was partly funded by a generous donation from the Society of St Vincent de Paul, together with a grant from special funds held by the Royal Academy. Bryan Neale was chosen by the Cathedral's Art and Architecture Committee from a number of artists who had submitted proposals. Following considerable research, particularly in the archives of the Daughters of Charity at Mill Hill, he produced the plaster sculpture from which the bronze was struck. The memorial reveals the determination, the compassion and the sense of humour of the saint, an appropriate presence in the Cathedral where so much stems from his inspiration. It was unveiled on his Feast Day, 27 September 1998.

On 10 July the following year, Bryan Neale's bronze relief of St Benedict of Nursia was unveiled. St Benedict is thought of as the father of Western monasticism. His Rule envisages the monk not as a solitary ascetic but as a brother among a family of brothers, serving God together. At his profession a monk takes lifelong vows of personal poverty, chastity and obedience to his abbot and the Rule, which sets out in detail how he should lead his life. When Benedict died, on 21 March 547, he had founded, without realizing it, an order which was to dominate monastic life in Europe for four centuries. It was a Benedictine, Pope Gregory the Great, who was inspired to evangelize England from Rome; they were Benedictines he sent, Benedictines who intellectually dominated the Synod of Whitby and Benedictines who kept the Christian faith and learning alive and active in England thereafter.

The bronze is also a tribute to our own Benedictine, Cardinal Hume, who died on 17 June 1999. He was insistent that St Benedict should be portrayed with the Rule which he himself followed from the age of 18. By the time he became Cardinal Archbishop of Westminster in 1976 he had spent 40 years of his life at Ampleforth, the Benedictine monastery in North Yorkshire, first as a schoolboy, then as a schoolmaster and monk and finally, from 1963, as Abbot. Like

St Benedict he had a deep understanding and compassion for the young, the weak and the vulnerable. He accepted people as they were; he did not condemn. Combining profound spirituality with disarming simplicity and honesty, he was able to defuse hostility and mollify resentment. It is appropriate that the only word that appears on the bronze, other than Benedict, is 'Pax'.

Some years ago Cardinal Hume appeared on television wearing slacks and a sweater in a programme about his beloved northern saints – Aidan and Cuthbert of Lindisfarne, Wilfred of York, Benedict Biscop and Bede of Wearmouth and Jarrow. He seemed relaxed and at home. Now they look down on him where he lies, at his own request, in the Chapel of St Gregory and St Augustine. High above hangs a red cardinal's hat made by a relative, Caroline Hickman. He is a Benedictine and is among Benedictines. But he was also Our Cardinal.

CARDINALS AND SCRIBES
THE CARDINAL ARCHBISHOPS OF WESTMINSTER

The addition of Cardinal Cormac Murphy-O'Connor's name to the list of Chief Pastors of the Catholic Church in England, draws attention to the long line of names which precedes it on the bronze plates near St Peter's statue, and is a reminder of the great events in English history in which so many of these men were directly concerned. But for some 300 years after the Reformation, England was administered from Rome and it was only in 1850, with the return of the Catholic Hierarchy, that local control was re-established. Since then there have been ten Cardinal Archbishops of Westminster. Their coats of arms can be found hewn in stone and marble, cast in bronze, carved and painted on wood and embroidered on liturgical vestments, throughout the Cathedral complex. The latest, that of Cardinal Cormac, bears the motto 'Gaudium et Spes' (Joy and hope).

Cardinal Nicholas Wiseman, First Archbishop of Westminster 1850-1865
Motto: 'Omnia pro Christo' (Everything for Christ). Born in Seville, Wiseman returned to the family home in Waterford on the death of his father, an Irish wine merchant. As a priest he loved both Rome and Ireland and made a triumphal tour of that country in 1858. At Westminster he established the structure of the diocese, using St Mary's, Moorfields, as his pro-cathedral, trebling the number both of priests and of churches, chapels and missions. He welcomed converts from Anglicanism and the vast number of Catholics who flooded into England from famine-stricken Ireland. In 1907 his body was transferred from Kensal Green cemetery, where he had been interred, to Westminster Cathedral and he lies now beneath the high altar in St Peter's Crypt.

Cardinal Henry Edward Manning, Second Archbishop of Westminster 1865-1892
Motto: 'Malo mori quam foedari' (I would rather die than compromise). Manning was born into the English upper class and educated at Harrow and Oxford. In 1851 he resigned his position as Anglican Archdeacon of Chichester and embraced Catholicism, subsequently concentrating on the provision of Catholic schools for the poor. He advocated social justice and supported trade unionism. In 1869 he transferred to the newly-built church of Our Lady of Victories, Kensington, as his pro-cathedral. For many years he directed financial resources to education but in 1884 he bought the site of Tothill Fields Prison on which Westminster Cathedral now stands. Interred at Kensal Green cemetery, in 1907 his body was transferred to St Peter's Crypt.

Cardinal Herbert Vaughan, Third Archbishop of Westminster 1892-1903
Motto: 'Amare et servire' (To love and to serve). From a deeply religious recusant family, Vaughan founded St Joseph's Missionary College at Mill Hill, the Catholic Missionary Society and the Catholic Truth Society. On his appointment to Westminster he set about funding and building a great cathedral there. He decided that Westminster Cathedral should be built in the Byzantine style and chose the architect, John Francis Bentley. The first major service in the newly-built Cathedral was his own Requiem Mass on 25 June 1903. Although a sarcophagus stands in the Vaughan Chantry near the Blessed Sacrament Chapel, with his coat of arms and cardinal's hat above, it is empty. Cardinal Vaughan's body lies, at his own request, at Mill Hill.

Cardinal Francis Bourne, Fourth Archbishop of Westminster 1903-1935
Motto: 'Ne cede malis' (Do not give in to evil). The son of a civil servant, Bourne was educated at St Edmund's, Ware, and became the first rector at Wonersh Seminary in Sussex. As Archbishop of Westminster he was responsible for much of the decoration we see today. Under Bourne the Cathedral was consecrated in 1910, the baldacchino, Stations of the Cross and present pulpit were erected, the Lady Chapel, St Andrew's Chapel, the Shrine of the Sacred Heart and the crypt were completed, and the marblework in the Blessed Sacrament Chapel, St Patrick's and St Paul's Chapels and the Vaughan Chantry installed. At his request, Cardinal Bourne's body lies at St Edmund's College, Ware.

Cardinal Arthur Hinsley, Fifth Archbishop of Westminster 1935-1943
Motto: 'Tales ambio defensores' (I gird myself with such defenders – a reference to St Thomas More and St John Fisher, canonized in 1935, the year of Hinsley's appointment). Born the son of a carpenter in 1865, Hinsley held the post of Rector of the Venerabile in Rome for 12 years and was then a missionary in Africa. Called out of retirement to be made Archbishop of Westminster, he initially tried to turn down the post. He saw World War II as a battle between good and evil, helping refugees and allied servicemen and becoming well known as a broadcaster. Because of the war, little work took place on decorating the Cathedral, but St Paul's Chapel received its Cosmatesque floor and the marblework in the Chapel of St Joseph, to whom Cardinal Hinsley was devoted, was installed. It is here that his body now lies.

Cardinal Bernard Griffin, Sixth Archbishop of Westminster 1943-1956
Motto: 'Da mihi animas' (Give me souls). The son of the manager of a bicycle-manufacturing company in Birmingham, Griffin served in the Royal Naval Air Service during World War I before being ordained. As Vicar-General and Auxiliary Bishop of the Birmingham diocese he was deeply committed to orphanages, youth and social work. While Archbishop of Westminster the marblework went up in the aisles and passages, St George's

Chapel received its altarpiece, the body of Bishop Challoner was interred in the Chapel of St Gregory and St Augustine and the medieval statue of Our Lady of Westminster was purchased at the cardinal's expense and installed below the Thirteenth Station of the Cross. His body lies in St Peter's Crypt.

Cardinal William Godfrey, Seventh Archbishop of Westminster 1956-1963
Motto: 'Pax a Deo' (Peace from God). Born in Liverpool into a staunchly Catholic family, Godfrey became Rector of the Venerabile and a Domestic Prelate to Pope Pius XI. He served on the Supreme Council for the Propagation of the Faith and on papal missions to Malta and Britain before becoming the first Apostolic Delegate to Britain. As Archbishop of Liverpool he scaled down the ambitious plans for a huge cathedral there to more realistic proportions. During his time as Archbishop of Westminster the Blessed Sacrament Chapel received its mosaics, the nave and narthex were clad with marble and the bronze of St Thérèse of Lisieux was put in place. He lies in St Peter's Crypt.

Cardinal John Carmel Heenan, Eighth Archbishop of Westminster 1963-1975
Motto: 'Sub umbra Carmeli' (Under the shadow of Carmel). Of Irish parents living in Ilford, he visited the Soviet Union and Nazi Germany before the war, reporting back to Cardinal Hinsley. In 1947 he re-established the Catholic Missionary Society. He became an accomplished broadcaster and presented the first High Mass on television. As Archbishop of Liverpool he instituted the final, radical, redesign of the new cathedral there. In the aftermath of the Second Vatican Council (1962-5), Heenan introduced the changes this brought in with considerable tact and diplomacy. Despite opposition, he was a staunch believer in ecumenism and formed a close personal friendship with the Archbishop of Canterbury, Dr Ramsey. In 1968 he welcomed him to Westminster Cathedral to preach and later that year he himself preached at Westminster Abbey. He lies, at his own request, below the Twelfth Station of the Cross.

Cardinal George Basil Hume OSB, Ninth Archbishop of Westminster 1976-1999
Motto: 'Pax inter spinas' (Peace among thorns). After spending most of his life at Ampleforth as schoolboy, monk, schoolmaster and finally Abbot, Cardinal Hume became Archbishop of Westminster in 1976. He put the Choir School, then threatened with closure, on a sound financial footing by the introduction of day-boys. In line with Vatican II he encouraged a greater use of the laity within the Church. He founded the Passage Day Centre, the Night Shelter and the Cardinal Hume Centre for the homeless and at risk. As archbishop he welcomed Pope John Paul II, the first reigning pontiff to visit Britain, in 1982, and Her Majesty the Queen, in the Cathedral's Centenary Year of 1995. She spoke of him as 'My Cardinal' and awarded him the Order of Merit shortly before his death. He lies in the Chapel of St Gregory and St Augustine.

OREMUS AND ITS PREDECESSORS

Oremus, the magazine of Westminster Cathedral, first appeared in January 1997. In a relatively short time it has recorded events such as the death of Cardinal Hume, the appointment of his successor, Cardinal Murphy-O'Connor, and the celebration of the Millennium Jubilee Year. But *Oremus* is in fact the sixth in a succession of magazines dealing with the life and times of the Cathedral.

The first was the *Westminster Cathedral Record*, started in January 1896 and selling at 6d a copy. This was intended primarily to encourage subscriptions to the Cathedral building fund. It contained regular progress reports by the architect, J F Bentley, accompanied by detailed scale drawings, together with lists of donations. Many of these were substantial – the Duke of Norfolk gave £10,000 (not far short of £500,000 today). Others paid for specific items in the Cathedral – a marble column cost from £50 while £33 bought 10,000 bricks. From 1899 the *Cathedral Record* was included as a supplement to *The Tablet*. Although intended to be produced quarterly, a total of only 11 issues of the *Cathedral Record* appeared, the last being in June 1902. By this time the architect was dead and a tribute to him from Cardinal Vaughan was included.

The cardinal himself died in June 1903 and for several years there was no Cathedral magazine. Then came the long-running *Westminster Cathedral Chronicle*, a monthly started in January 1907 at 2d a copy or 3/- a year, post paid. By now, of course, the Cathedral was up and running and the *Cathedral Chronicle* was less concerned with fundraising. Its 34 pages, complete with black-and-white photographs and advertisements, contained addresses from the archbishop, details of appointments and departures from Clergy House, articles on the liturgy, reports on the decoration of the Cathedral, on cathedrals elsewhere, on events in Rome, stories, poetry and a list of services and other events in the Cathedral.

The *Cathedral Chronicle* ran for just over 60 years. It duly recorded the consecration of the Cathedral in 1910 and the succession of four new cardinals during the period. When it started the Cathedral was almost entirely bare brick. When it ceased the marble and mosaic to be seen today were largely in place. The magazine continued to be produced during World War I which, except for a paper shortage, affected the Cathedral remarkably little, and World War II which affected it much more. The Cathedral closed early because of the black-out, protective scaffolding surrounded the marble columns and baldacchino while bombs blew in windows and scarred the woodwork.

The last issue of the *Cathedral Chronicle* was in December 1967. The period following the Second Vatican Council and the changes it introduced was a very difficult one for the Church. Meanwhile the production costs of the *Cathedral Chronicle*, then priced at 1/-, had soared, requiring an annual subsidy from Cathedral funds of £600. A cheaper monthly magazine, the *Westminster Cathedral News Sheet*, more ecumenical in tone, appeared in January 1968 at a price of 6d. Initially consisting of eight pages, it was published without the in-depth articles and photographs of the *Cathedral Chronicle*, though addresses from the archbishop, a meditation, new appointments, the diary and the list of Cathedral services remained.

The *Cathedral News Sheet* lasted for only 40 issues. In May 1971 the very similar eight-page *Westminster Cathedral Journal* appeared at the same price, with the explanation that 'for some time many readers have felt that the old title was incongruous, and we hope that the *Cathedral Journal* will go on to increase in interest and literary merit'. But its life was even shorter than the *Cathedral News Sheet*, the last issue being in December 1973. Although it had increased in price to 10p at the start of 1972, the reason given for its demise, as with the *Cathedral Chronicle*, was that production required a considerable subsidy from Cathedral funds which the Cathedral, faced with stringent economies at this time, could no longer afford.

Such was the inauspicious situation in 1974 when the *Westminster Cathedral Bulletin* was born. Initially of one or two sides of typewritten foolscap it necessarily contained little more than service times and the Cathedral diary. It was produced fortnightly, for the four years from October 1979 by members of the (now defunct) Parish Council, and it was free. Against all the odds the *Cathedral Bulletin* not only survived but prospered and gradually expanded, to contain features on major events such as the Pope's visit to Ireland in 1979. In April 1981 a charge of 5p was levied and the following September it became a monthly, with more expensive special issues being produced for major events such the Pope's visit to the Cathedral in 1982 and (under the title *Westminster Cathedral Journal*) at Christmas 1982 and Easter 1983 and 1984.

The *Westminster Cathedral Bulletin* underwent several metamorphoses, a new format being introduced in 1979 and again in 1985 and 1992. Over the years since it first appeared the *Cathedral Bulletin* changed from being a rather scruffy typewritten sheet of paper to a fully-fledged 12-page monthly magazine on glossy paper, containing articles, interviews, photographs, a cartoon (Charlie Chaplin) and advertisements, as well as all the material previously provided concerning the Cathedral. As the 1990s progressed there was increasing use of colour in the design of the front cover, and occasionally colour photographs as well, particularly when special issues were produced, such as that to commemorate HM the Queen's historic visit to the Cathedral in 1995.

In 1996 a wide-ranging review of the *Cathedral Bulletin* was carried out. A survey of readers demonstrated the popularity of the magazine but suggested more photographs, more colour and greater coverage of Cathedral and parish news, suggestions which have been incorporated in subsequent issues. It was also felt that the name itself, suggesting the rapid transmission of news, was inappropriate. Ideas for a new title included the *Chronicle*, the *Tower*, and the *Bell*. Charlie Chaplain suggested *Halo Magazine*! What was needed was something illustrating the atmosphere and special character of the Cathedral. After much discussion the title finally agreed upon was '*Oremus*, The Magazine of Westminster Cathedral'. For 'Oremus' means 'Let us pray' in Latin and it is prayer which unites all those who worship here and the prayerful atmosphere of the Cathedral which our many visitors find so noticeable and so welcoming.

SOURCES

CREATION AND SURVIVAL

Before the Cathedral
Henry Mayhew, *The Criminal Prisons of London*, Griffin, 1862; *Westminster Cathedral Chronicle*, Aug. and Sept. 1910; Winefride de l'Hôpital, *Westminster Cathedral and its Architect*, Hutchinson, 1919; Weinreb and Hibbert, *London Encyclopaedia*, 1983; maps of Westminster dated 1746, 1799, 1819, 1883, 1919.

The choir that never was
The Tablet, 6.7.1895, 13.5.99, 29.12.00, 7.6.02; Winefride de l'Hôpital, *Westminster Cathedral and its Architect*, Hutchinson, 1919; Shane Leslie, *Letters of Herbert Cardinal Vaughan to Lady Herbert of Lea*, Burns & Oates, 1942; A S G Butler, *John Francis Bentley*, Burns & Oates, 1961; Rene Kollar, *Westminster Cathedral: From Dream to Reality*, Edinburgh, 1987; Peter Doyle, *Westminster Cathedral 1895-1995*, Geoffrey Chapman, 1995.

The lost sea of Westminster
Westminster Cathedral Record, 2.1899; Norwich Union Insurance Company Minutes, 6.12.01; *The Tablet*, 7.6.02; *Catholic Herald*, 14.8.03; *Architectural Review*, 1.08; W G Renwick, *Marble and Marble Working*, London, 1909; Winefride de l'Hôpital, *Westminster Cathedral and its Architect*, Hutchinson, 1919; Edward Skipper, *Celebrating Skipper 1880-1980*; Stefan Muthesius, *The Marble Hall: G J Skipper and the Norwich Union*; Norwich Union brochures, 'Surrey House', 'Inside Surrey House', 'The Surrey House Marble'; Corporation of London, *Guide to the Old Bailey*, 1992; Cathedral architectural drawings, F-52, 86, 87.

The Great Rood
Westminster Cathedral Record, 1.1896; *The Tablet* 7.6.02, 19.12.03; Letters from Vaughan to Symons 22.2.03, 10.3.03, 3.4.03; Winefride de l'Hôpital, *Westminster Cathedral and its Architect*, Hutchinson, 1919; *Westminster Cathedral Chronicle*, 1.34, 2.37; Ernest Oldmeadow, *Francis Cardinal Bourne*, Burns, Oates and Washbourne, 1944; *Westminster Year Book* (photo), 1995; Cathedral architectural drawings, A-8, B-22, 23, 24, 25, 26, 34, F-84.

Let there be light
Lethaby and Swainson, *The Church of Sancta Sophia, Constantinople*, Macmillan, 1894; *Westminster Cathedral Record*, 7.96, 10.96; *The Tablet*, 29.12.00; *Westminster Cathedral Chronicle*, 12.10; Winefride de l'Hôpital, *Westminster Cathedral and its Architect*, Hutchinson, 1919; A S G Butler, *John Francis Bentley*, Burns & Oates, 1961.

The Cathedral in wartime
Westminster Cathedral Chronicle, 10.17, 2.18, 10.39, 11.39, 5.41, 9.43, 9.45, 11.45 (L H Shattock, 'The Cathedral and the Blitz'), 6.46, 5.49; *Westminster Cathedral News Sheet*, 12.68; *Westminster Cathedral Bulletin*, 5.92, 12.93.

FROM DARKNESS TO LIGHT

The unknown architect
Observer, 17.10.15; *The Builder*, 5.11.15; *Westminster Cathedral Chronicle*, 12.15, 1.22, 6.24, 1.27 (Obituary), 1.34; Winefride de l'Hôpital, *Westminster Cathedral and its Architect*, Hutchinson, 1919; Robert Speaight, *The Life of Eric Gill*, Methuen, 1966; Eric Gill, *Autobiography*, Lund Humphries, 1992; Cathedral architectural drawings, D-1 folder, D-65, E-5 folder, F-11 folder, F-99, 100, H-8, 35.

Salve et vale
The Tablet, 7.6.1902; Winefride de l'Hôpital, *Westminster*

Cathedral and its Architect, Hutchinson, 1919; *Westminster Cathedral Chronicle*, 7.18, 3.25, 5.63; *Westminster Cathedral Bulletin*, 5.63; John Browne and Tim Dean, *Westminster Cathedral: Building of Faith*, Booth-Clibborn, 1995.

The start of the journey
The Tablet, 7.6.1902; *Westminster Cathedral Chronicle*, 12.07, 3.09, 10.13, 9.16, 8.25, 2.27, 9.47, 11.48, 3.67; Winefride de l'Hôpital, *Westminster Cathedral and its Architect*, Hutchinson, 1919; *Westminster Cathedral News Sheet*, 3.69, 6.69; *Westminster Cathedral Journal*, 6.72; Cathedral architectural drawings, E-10, 11, 12.

Shamrocks and snakes
Westminster Cathedral Chronicle, 6.10, 7.23, 8.24, 11.24, 12.27, 3.28, 7.28, 9.28, 11.28, 2.29, 6.29, 9.30, 6.39, 1.51, 6.60, 3.61; Winefride de l'Hôpital, *Westminster Cathedral and its Architect*, Hutchinson, 1919; CTS Cathedral Guidebooks, 1957 and 1965; *Oremus*, 7/8.98, 4.99; Cathedral architectural drawings, D-6 folder, D-16, 32B, 36C, 39E, 49F.

Contemplation, sorrow and prayer
Westminster Cathedral Chronicle, 3.09, 10.13, 12.15, 9.16, 2.18, 3.18, 4.18; Eric Gill drawings 1920-12-11-1 dated Spring 1914 (British Museum); *The Universe*, letters 30.7.15 – 5.11.15; *Observer*, articles 3.10.15 and 17.10.15, letters 17.10.15 – 28.11.15; *The Builder*, 5.11.15; Winefride de l'Hôpital, *Westminster Cathedral and its Architect*, Hutchinson, 1919; Robert Speaight, *The Life of Eric Gill*, Methuen, 1966; *The New Catholic Encyclopaedia*, McGraw-Hill, 1967; Malcolm Yorke, *Eric Gill, Man of Flesh and Spirit*, Constable, 1981; David Peace, *Westminster Cathedral Friends Newsletters*, Autumn 1985, Spring 1986; Fiona MacCarthy, *Eric Gill*, Faber and Faber, 1989; Eric Gill, *Autobigraphy*, Lund Humphries, 1992; Cathedral architectural drawings (George Daniels sketches), C-5 folder.

The three pulpits
Westminster Cathedral Record, 1.1896, 4.96; *The Tablet*, 7.6.02; *Catholic Herald*, 12.6.03; *Westminster Cathedral Chronicle*, 5.14,

6.29, 1.34, 9.34, 10.34; Winefride de l'Hôpital, *Westminster Cathedral and its Architect*, Hutchinson, 1919; Ernest Oldmeadow, *Francis Cardinal Bourne*, Burns, Oates and Washbourne, 1944; Peter Doyle, *Westminster Cathedral 1895-1995*, Geoffrey Chapman, 1995; Cathedral architectural drawings, H-35, 37, 13696.

Our Lady of Walsingham and the missing Gospels
H Philibert Feasey, *Our Ladye of Walsingham*, 1901; *Westminster Cathedral Chronicle*, 4.34, 8.34, 9.34, 8.64; *The Universe*, 20.7.34; *Illustrated London News*, 18.8.34; *Catholic Herald*, 14.3.47; J C Dickinson, *The Shrine of Our Lady of Walsingham*, CUP, 1956; H M Gillett, *Shrines of Our Lady in England and Wales*, Samuel Walker, 1957; Dominic Pyle-Bridges, *Guide to the Sanctuary of Our Lady of Walsingham*, 1974; *Walsingham Newsletter*, 8.92; Peter Cobb, *Walsingham*.

Our Lady of Westminster
Philip Nelson, *The Archaeological Journal*, 1925; A Rostand, *Les Albâtres Anglais du XVe Siècle en Basse-Normandie*, 1928; W. L. Hildburgh, *Antiquaries Journal*, 1937; W L Hildburgh, *Burlington Magazine*, 1946, 1955; *Connoisseur*, June 1955; *The Tablet*, 10.12.55; *Westminster Cathedral Chronicle*, 12.55; H M Gillett, *Shrines of Our Lady in England and Wales*, Samuel Walker, 1957; Francis Cheetham, *Medieval English Alabaster Carvings*, Nottingham, 1973; Musée d'Aquitaine, *Sculpture Médiévale de Bordeaux et du Bordelais*, 1976; Francis Cheetham, *English Medieval Alabasters*, Oxford, 1984; Leigh and Podmore, *Outstanding Churches in Craven*, 1985; *Westminster Cathedral Bulletin*, 11.95; *Sculptures d'Albâtre du Moyen Age*, Rouen, 1998; *Les Sculptures Anglaises d'Albâtre*, Cluny Museum, Paris, 1998; Letter from Brimo de Larroussilhe, Paris, 28.5.99; *Guide to All Saints Church*, Broughton-in-Craven.

A still point in a turning world
Westminster Cathedral Chronicle, 1.07, 5.07, 8.07, 2.08, 1.09, 7.09, 5.14, 5.56; Winefride de l'Hôpital, *Westminster Cathedral and its Architect*, Hutchinson, 1919; a Mill Hill Father,

Remembered in Blessing: The Courtfield Story, Sands, 1955; Mgr Gordon Wheeler, *The Blessed Sacrament Chapel Mosaics*, 1962; Cathedral architectural drawings, C-8, 11.

CATHEDRAL MARBLES

The marble seekers

London Post Office Directory (Streets and Trades), entries for Farmer and Brindley 1863, 65, 68, 81, 83, 85, 87, 88, 96, 99, 1908, 24, 29; Charles Garnier, *Le Nouvel Opéra de Paris*, Paris, 1878; R L Playfair, Blue Book of Consular Reports (France, Algiers), 1881; R L Playfair, *Proceedings of the British Association* (Geological Section K), 1885; William Brindley, *RIBA Transactions*, 1887, 88, 94-5, 96-7, 1902-3, 07; Lethaby and Swainson, *The Church of Sancta Sophia, Constantinople*, Macmillan, 1894; *Westminster Cathedral Record*, 2.99; W G Renwick, *Marble and Marble Working*, London, 1909; *The Builder*, 14.3.19 (Brindley obituary); Winefride de l'Hôpital, *Westminster Cathedral and its Architect*, Hutchinson, 1919; *Westminster Cathedral Chronicle*, 10.19, 1.22, 3.24, 9.28; Farmer and Brindley, company records, 1929; Stephen Bayley, *The Albert Memorial*, Scholar Press, 1981; Benedict Read, *Victorian Sculpture*, Yale UP, 1982; *County Hall*, Athlone, 1991; Opéra National de Paris, *Visite de l'Opéra Palais Garnier*; Farmer and Brindley, references in Nikolaus Pevsner *et al*, 'The Buildings of England' series; Cathedral architectural drawings, B-23, 25, 28, 31, 40, C-8, 11, 50, 52, 55, D-5, 9, 16, 68, 83, 88, F-65, H-4, 15.

Cipollino

Pliny the Elder, *Natural History*, Book 36.48-9; Charles Garnier, *Le Nouvel Opéra de Paris*, Paris, 1878; Farmer and Brindley in London Post Office Directory (Trades) 1881, 85, 99, 1908; William Brindley, *RIBA Transactions* 1887, 94-5, 1907; Lethaby and Swainson, *The Church of Sancta Sophia, Constantinople*, Macmillan, 1894; *Westminster Cathedral Record*, 2.99; *The Tablet*, 13.5.99, 29.12.1900; Farmer and Brindley, company records, 1905; Mary Winearls Porter, *What Rome was built with*, London, 1907; John Watson, *British and Foreign Marbles and other Ornamental*

Stones, Cambridge, 1916; Winefride de l'Hôpital, *Westminster Cathedral and its Architect*, Hutchinson, 1919; *Westminster Cathedral Chronicle*, 3.56, 9/10.59, 12.60; J B Ward-Perkins, *Marble in Antiquity*, British School at Rome, 1992; Yannis Maniatis, *The Study of Marble and other Stones used in Antiquity*, Archetype, 1995; information from Aelred Bartlett, 2000-2; field trip to Karystos and Kylindroi Quarry on Mount Ocha, May 2003.

The lost columns

John Ruskin, *The Stones of Venice*, Dent, 1851; *Westminster Cathedral Record*, 2.99; *The Tablet*, 13.5.99, 29.12.1900, 7.6.02; Winefride de l'Hôpital, *Westminster Cathedral and its Architect*, Hutchinson, 1919; Henry Tristram, *Cardinal Newman and the Church of Birmingham Oratory*, Birmingham, 1934; *Westminster Cathedral Chronicle*, 5.49; Paul Chavasse, *The Birmingham Oratory Church*; Cathedral architectural drawing, F-65.

Verde Antico

William Brindley, *RIBA Transactions*, 1887, 94-5, 96-7, 1907; Lethaby and Swainson, *The Church of Sancta Sophia, Constantinople*, Macmillan, 1894; London Post Office Directory (Trades), 1896, 1907, 1913; *Illustrated London News*, 24.4.1897–11.6.98; *Westminster Cathedral Record*, 2.99; *The Tablet*, 13.5.99, 29.12.1900; W G Renwick, *Marble and Marble Working*, London, 1909; John Watson, *British and Foreign Marbles and other Ornamental Stones*, Cambridge, 1916; Winefride de l'Hôpital, *Westminster Cathedral and its Architect*, Hutchinson, 1919; *Westminster Cathedral Chronicle*, 4.32, 5.63, 8.63, 7.64; J B Ward-Perkins, *Marble in Antiquity*, British School at Rome, 1992; Zane Katsikis, *Greece by Rail*, Bradt, 1997; information from Tsalmas Melas of Tsalmas Marmi/Tsalma Marble, Larissa, May 2000, May 2003; field trip to Larissa and verde antico quarries below Mount Ossa, May 2003.

Rosso antico

RIBA Transactions, 1869; *The Times* (Byron Memorial), 27.5.1880, 8.12.1880; Farmer and Brindley in London Post Office Directory (Trades), 1887, 1899, 1908; W G Renwick, *Marble and Marble*

SOURCES

Working, London, 1909; *Westminster Cathedral Chronicle*, 12.60; Frederick Cooper, 'The Quarries of Mount Taygetos in the Peloponnesos, Greece', in Herz and Waelkens, *Classical Marble: Geochemistry, Technology, Trade*, Kluwer, 1988; Lorenzo Lazzarini, *Rosso Antico and other Red Marbles used in Antiquity*, J Paul Getty Museum, Malibu, CA, 1990; J B Ward-Perkins, *Marble in Antiquity*, British School at Rome, 1992; Gabriele Borghini, *Marmi Antichi*, Edizioni De Luca, Rome, 1998; Patrizio Pensabene, *Il Marmo e il Colore*, Rome, 1998; field trip to Paganea, Cape Tenaro and Profitis Ilias quarries, May 2000.

Purple porphyry

William Brindley, *RIBA Transactions*, 1887, 88; *The Builder*, 12.11.1887; Farmer and Brindley in London Post Office Directory (Trades), 1888, 1908; Lethaby and Swainson, *The Church of Sancta Sophia, Constantinople*, Macmillan, 1894; Mary Winearls Porter, *What Rome was built with*, London, 1907; John Watson, *British and Foreign Marbles and other Ornamental Stones*, Cambridge, 1916; *Westminster Cathedral Chronicle*, 9.28; David Meredith, *Journal of Egyptian Archaeology*, 1952; Giorgio Vasari, *Vasari on Technique*, Dover, 1960; J B Ward-Perkins, *Marble in Antiquity*, British School at Rome, 1992; Stephen Bann, *The Sculpture of Stephen Cox*, 1995; Suzanne Butters, *The Triumph of Vulcan*, Leo S Olschki, 1996; *21st Century British Sculpture* 'Stephen Cox', 2002.

Carrara

Pliny the Elder, *Natural History*, Book 36.48; Mary Winearls Porter, *What Rome was built with*, London, 1907; W G Renwick, *Marble and Marble Working*, London, 1909; Winefride de l'Hôpital, *Westminster Cathedral and its Architect*, Hutchinson, 1919; Giorgio Vasari, *Vasari on Technique*, Dover, 1960; Cathy Newman, 'Carrara Marble', *National Geographic*, 7.82; Luciana and Tiziano Mannoni, *Marble -- The History of a Culture*, Facts on File, 1985; J B Ward-Perkins, *Marble in Antiquity*, British School at Rome, 1992; Yannis Maniatis, *The Study of Marble and other Stones used in Antiquity*, Archetype, 1995; field trip to Carrara and Fantiscritti quarries, September 2000.

Cork red

Henry Kinahan, *Economic Geology of Ireland*, RGSI, 1886-7; John Watson, *British and Foreign Marbles and other Ornamental Stones*, Cambridge, 1916; Winefride de l'Hôpital, *Westminster Cathedral and its Architect*, Hutchinson, 1919; W E Nevill, *Geological Magazine*, 12.12.62; Patrick Wyse Jackson, *The Building Stones of Dublin*, Country House, 1993; Geological Survey of Ireland (GSI), MinLocs Database and Maps; GSI Mineral Resources Research Unit – Site Report (Baneshane), 28.3.88; A G Sleeman, *Geology of South Cork*; Colin Rynne, *The Industrial Archaeology of Cork City and its Environs*; *Sunday Telegraph*, 22.1.95; information from Maighread Hyde, Midleton, Co Cork, and Aelred Bartlett, 2000-2; field trip to Baneshane, Midleton and Little Island quarries, April 2002.

Connemara green

Mr and Mrs S C Hall, *Ireland*, Hall, Virtue and Co, London, 1843 pp.462-4; Henry Kinahan, *Economic Geology of Ireland*, RGSI, 1886-7; John Watson, *British and Foreign Marbles and other Ornamental Stones*, Cambridge, 1916; Winefride de l'Hôpital, *Westminster Cathedral and its Architect*, Hutchinson, 1919; Michael Max, *Connemara Marble and the Industry based upon it*, GSI, 1985; E Naughton, *The Assessment of Connemara Marble Resources*, 1992; Kathleen Villiers-Tuthill, *The History of Clifden*, 1992; Patrick Wyse Jackson, *The Building Stones of Dublin*, Country House, 1993; *Directory of Active Quarries, Pits and Mines in Ireland*, GSI, 1994; Connemara Marble Industries brochures; information from Ambrose Joyce (father and son), Moycullen, Co Galway, and Mark Joyce, Recess, Co Galway, June 2002; field trip to Streamstown, Barnanoraun, and Lissoughter quarries, June 2002.

Iona green

The Builder, 10.12.15; *Westminster Cathedral Chronicle*, 12.15; Winefride de l'Hôpital, *Westminster Cathedral and its Architect*, Hutchinson, 1919; E M MacArthur, *Iona 1750-1914*, 1990; David Viner, *The Iona Marble Quarry*, New Iona Press, 1992; Anna Ritchie, *Historic Scotland – Iona*, 1997; field trips to Iona marble quarry, July 1997, August 1998, July 2002.

Derbyshire fossil and Hopton Wood
Arthur Lee, *Marble and Marble Workers*, Crosby Lockwood, 1888; W G Renwick, *Marble and Marble Working*, London, 1909; John Watson, *British and Foreign Marbles and other Ornamental Stones*, Cambridge, 1916; *Westminster Cathedral Chronicle*, 7.18, 5.26, 4.29; Winefride de l'Hôpital, *Westminster Cathedral and its Architect*, Hutchinson, 1919; Malcolm Yorke, *Eric Gill, Man of Flesh and Spirit*, Constable, 1981; John Browne and Tim Dean, *Westminster Cathedral: Building of Faith*, Booth-Clibborn, 1995; Ian Thomas, *Tarmac's Derbyshire Heritage*, The Tarmac Papers, 2000; Cathedral architectural drawings; information from Ian Thomas, Director of the National Stone Centre, and Francis Lowe of Francis N Lowe Ltd, Middleton, Derbyshire; field trip to Coalhills, Dene and Wirksworth quarries, November 2001.

A tour of the marbles
Westminster Cathedral Record (supplement to *The Tablet*), 29.12.1900; John Watson, *British and Foreign Marbles and other Ornamental Stones*, Cambridge, 1916; Winefride de l'Hôpital, *Westminster Cathedral and its Architect*, Hutchinson, 1919; *Westminster Cathedral Chronicle*; Francis Bartlett, annotated photographs of the Cathedral marbles, 1950-6; Francis Bartlett, *Westminster Cathedral Friends Newsletters*, Spring and Autumn, 1989; J B Ward-Perkins, *Marble in Antiquity*, British School at Rome, 1992; *Westminster Cathedral Bulletin*, 5.95, 6.95; Cathedral architectural drawings; information from Gerald Culliford of Gerald Culliford Ltd, Ian MacDonald of McMarmilloyd Ltd, Henry Buckley and Dave Smith of the Natural History Museum in London, Monica Price of the University Museum of Natural History at Oxford and Tom Heldal of Norway's Geological Survey, Trondheim.

CATHEDRAL MOSAICS

Mosaics and methods
The Universe, 25.4.1903, 5.1.34; *Westminster Gazette*, 29.4.03; *Catholic Herald*, 1.5.03; *Westminster Cathedral Chronicle*, 4.11,

11.11, 2.12, 1.13, 8.14, 12.15, 4.16, 9.16, 1.22, 8.24, 5.27, 7.27, 1.28, 1.30, 4.30, 1.32, 3.32, 1.34, 2.34, 8.34, 10.34, 7.35, 4.50, 8.52, 5.56, 7.58, 4.61, 8.61, 1.62, 2.62, 8.62, 2.65; Order Book of James Powell and Sons 1915-16; Winefride de l'Hôpital, *Westminster Cathedral and its Architect*, Hutchinson, 1919; *Catholic Times*, 5.2.32, 10.8.34; Giorgio Vasari, *Vasari on Technique*, Dover, 1960; Mgr Gordon Wheeler, *The Blessed Sacrament Chapel Mosaics*, 1962; *Westminster Cathedral Bulletin*, 9.82; Justin Vulliamy, *Westminster Cathedral Friends Newsletter*, Autumn 1987; Manuela Farneti, *Glossario Tecnico-Storico del Mosaico*, Longo Editore, Ravenna, 1993; Peter Doyle, *Westminster Cathedral 1895-1995*, Geoffrey Chapman, 1995; John Browne and Tim Dean, *Westminster Cathedral: Building of Faith*, Booth-Clibborn, 1995; C M Ravenna, *I Colori della Luce*, Marsilio Editori, Venezia, 1996; Roger Ling, *Ancient Mosaics*, British Museum Press, 1998; Elaine Goodwin, *The Art of Decorative Mosaics*, Crowood, 1999; *Oremus*, 4.99, 7/8.01, 6.02, 12.02; information from Aelred Bartlett, 2000-2.

Not Angles but Angels
J R Green, *A Short History of the English People*, Macmillan 1902; *Westminster Cathedral Chronicle*, 11.07, 7.28; Winefride de l'Hôpital, *Westminster Cathedral and its Architect*, Hutchinson, 1919; S and E Usherwood, *Friends Newsletter*, Spring, 1992.

The blue altarpiece
The Tablet, 21.3.03; Winefride de l'Hôpital, *Westminster Cathedral and its Architect*, Hutchinson, 1919; *Westminster Cathedral Chronicle*, 1.13, 2.13, 4.13, 1.34.

I am the gate
Westminster Cathedral Record, 10.1896; *The Tablet*, 29.12.1900; *Westminster Cathedral Chronicle*, 3.07, 4.16, 1.34; Winefride de l'Hôpital, *Westminster Cathedral and its Architect*, Hutchinson, 1919.

The lost mosaic
Westminster Cathedral Chronicle, 8.23, 3.26, 7.27, 4.30, 1.32, 10.33, 1.34, 2.34, 8.34, 11.36; *Catholic Times*, 5.2.32, 10.8.34, 6.12.35; *Daily Telegraph*, 7.12.33, 4.12.35; *The Universe*, 5.1.34, 6.12.35; *Manchester Guardian*, 3.12.35; *Evening Standard*, 3.12.35; Peter

SOURCES

Doyle, *Westminster Cathedral 1895-1995*, Geoffrey Chapman, 1995; information from Jane Buxton (Gilbert Pownall's daughter), 1995-6.

The host of heaven and the missing apostle
Westminster Cathedral Chronicle, 1.32, 10.33, 1.34; *New Catholic Encyclopaedia*, McGraw-Hill, 1967.

In the footsteps of St Paul
Westminster Cathedral Chronicle, 8.61, 8.62, 3.64, 4.64, 2.65; *Westminster Cathedral Friends Newsletter*, Autumn 1987; Peter Doyle, *Westminster Cathedral 1895-1995*, Geoffrey Chapman, 1995; John Browne and Tim Dean, *Westminster Cathedral: Building of Faith*, Booth-Clibborn, 1995; information from Aelred Bartlett, 2000-2.

ANIMALS AND ANGELS

Thomas More's monkey
Westminster Cathedral Chronicle, 7.40, 2.47, 3.48; *Catholic Times*, 24.12.43; *Catholic Herald*, letters 7.2.47, 14.2.47, 7.3.47, 14.3.47, 21.3.47; Robert Speaight, *The Life of Eric Gill*, Methuen, 1966; Malcolm Yorke, *Eric Gill, Man of Flesh and Spirit*, Constable, 1981; Fiona MacCarthy, *Eric Gill*, Faber & Faber, 1989; *Westminster Cathedral Bulletin*, 6.92, 11.95; Judith Collins, *Eric Gill: Sculpture*, Lund Humphries with the Barbican Art Gallery, 1992; John Guy, *Thomas More*, Edward Arnold, 2000; drawing of altarpiece (with monkey), reference UCLA EG 312-314, dated 20-26.7.39, held by William Andrews Clark Memorial Library, University of California, Los Angeles; drawing of altarpiece (with monkey) inscribed 'Westminster Cath. St George's Chapel, reredos (revised dr.) 1/8 full size E.G. 29.7.39', held by John Skelton (Eric Gill's nephew).

MEMORIALS AND MARTYRS

St John Southworth: The story of the body
Albert Purdie, *The Life of Blessed John Southworth, Priest and Martyr*, Burns, Oates and Washbourne 1930; *Westminster*

Cathedral Chronicle, 6.30, 8.30, 1.55; Godfrey Anstruther, *A Hundred Homeless Years*, Blackfriars, 1958; *British Catholics in Douai*, Musée de la Chartreuse, Douai.

The Russian in the crypt
The Tablet, 16.12.16, 23.12.16, 20.1.17, 27.1.17, 7.4.17; *The Times*, 12.1.17, 15.1.17, 16.1.17, 23.1.17; *Westminster Cathedral Chronicle*, 2.17, 3.40; *Westminster Cathedral Bulletin*, 7/8.93; Sheila Fitzpatrick, *The Russian Revolution*, OUP, 1994.

Our Lady of Vilna
Westminster Cathedral Chronicle, 4.44; *International Geographic Encyclopaedia and Atlas*, Columbia University Press, 1975; John Browne and Tim Dean, *Westminster Cathedral: Building of Faith*, Booth-Clibborn, 1995; *Columbia Gazetteer of the World*, Columbia University Press, 1998; Gordon McLachlan, *Lithuania*, Bradt Travel Guides, 2002.

Per ardua ad astra
Westminster Cathedral Chronicle, 9.47, 10.67; *Westminster Cathedral Newssheet* 3.69, 6.69, 7.69; *Westminster Cathedral Journal*, 6.72; Joann Cerrito, *Contemporary Artists*, St James, 1996.

Along the way
Westminster Cathedral Chronicle, 11.49, 4.50, 7.58; Robert Maillard, *A Dictionary of Modern Sculpture*, Methuen, 1962; *Westminster Cathedral Friends Newsletter*, Spring 1984; *Westminster Cathedral Bulletin*, 11.93; Joann Cerrito, *Contemporary Artists*, St James, 1996.

St Vincent and St Benedict
New Catholic Encyclopaedia, McGraw-Hill, 1967; Donald Attwater, *Penguin Dictionary of Saints*, Penguin, 1993; *Oremus*, 7/8.98, 11.98, 7/8.99, 9.99, 10.99, 11.99; *The Monastery of St Benedict*, Subiaco, 2001.

CARDINALS AND SCRIBES

The Cardinal Archbishops of Westminster
Ernest Oldmeadow, *Francis Cardinal Bourne*, Burns, Oates and

Washbourne, 1940/44; John Heenan, *Cardinal Hinsley*, Burns, Oates and Washbourne, 1944; Michael de la Bedoyère, *Cardinal Bernard Griffin*, Rockliffe, 1955; *Westminster Cathedral Chronicle* (Cardinal Godfrey obituary), 3.63; Cardinal John Heenan, *Not the Whole Truth*, 1971, *Crown of Thorns*, 1974, Hodder and Stoughton; Richard Schiefen, *Nicholas Wiseman and the Transformation of English Catholicism*, Patmos, 1984; Robert Gray, *Cardinal Manning*, Weidenfeld and Nicolson, 1985; Thomas Moloney, *Westminster, Whitehall and the Vatican – The Role of Cardinal Hinsley*, Burns and Oates, 1985; Robert O'Neil, *Cardinal Herbert Vaughan*, Burns and Oates, 1995; S. and E. Usherwood, *Westminster Cathedral Friends Newsletters*, Spring and Autumn 1997, Spring 1998; *Oremus*, Nov. 2000 – Feb. 2001.